UTAH
BEACH

The 'Battle Zone Normandy' Series

Orne Bridgehead Lloyd Clark

Sword Beach Ken Ford

Juno Beach Ken Ford

Gold Beach Simon Trew

Omaha Beach Tim Bean

Utah Beach Stephen Badsey

Villers-Bocage George Forty

Battle for Cherbourg Robin Havers

Operation Epsom Lloyd Clark

Battle for St-Lô Nigel de Lee

Battle for Caen Simon Trew

Operation Cobra Christopher Pugsley

Road to Falaise Steve Hart

Falaise Pocket Paul Latawski

All of these titles can be ordered via the
Sutton Publishing website
www.suttonpublishing.co.uk

**The 'Battle Zone Normandy'
Editorial and Design Team**

Series Editor Simon Trew

Senior Commissioning Editor Jonathan Falconer

Assistant Editor Nick Reynolds

Cover and Page Design Martin Latham

Editing and Layout Donald Sommerville

Mapping Map Creation Ltd

Photograph Scanning and Mapping Bow Watkinson

Index Michael Forder

BATTLE
ZONE
NORMANDY

UTAH BEACH

STEPHEN BADSEY

Series Editor: Simon Trew

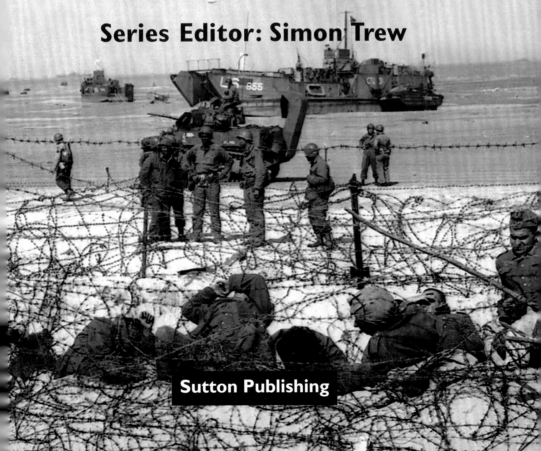

Sutton Publishing

First Published in 2004 by
Sutton Publishing Limited · Phoenix Mill
Thrupp · Stroud · Gloucestershire · GL5 2BU

British Library Cataloguing in Publication Data
A catalogue record for this book is available
from The British Library.

ISBN 0-7509-3013-6

Typeset in 10.5/14 pt Sabon

Printed and bound in England by
J.H. Haynes & Co. Ltd, Sparkford

Front cover: Troops coming ashore on Utah Beach on D-Day. *(US National Archives [USNA])*

Page 1: Part of the WN-5/WN-104 defences on Utah Beach, a concrete pit fitted with a 50-mm anti-tank gun. Most of the WN-5 complex is still visible among the dunes. *(Author)*

Page 3: Soldiers of VII Corps look on as German prisoners rest in a barbed wire enclosure on Utah Beach after being interrogated, 6 June 1944. *(USNA)*

Page 7: Men of 8th Infantry Regiment, among the first waves to land at Utah Beach on D-Day, taking cover behind the sea wall before moving out. *(USNA)*

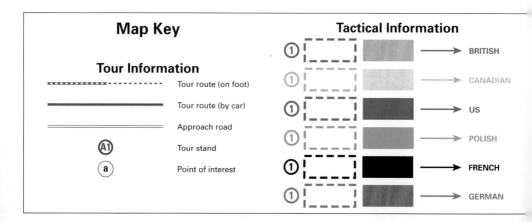

Map Key

Tour Information

.... Tour route (on foot)

—————————————— Tour route (by car)

══════════════ Approach road

(A1) Tour stand

(a) Point of interest

Tactical Information

① ⌐ ⌐ ▭ ———→ BRITISH

① ⌐ ⌐ ▭ ———→ CANADIAN

① ⌐ ⌐ ▭ ———→ US

① ⌐ ⌐ ▭ ———→ POLISH

① ⌐ ⌐ ▭ ———→ FRENCH

① ⌐ ⌐ ▭ ———→ GERMAN

CONTENTS

PART ONE
INTRODUCTION 7

Battle Zone Normandy   *Dr Simon Trew*   8

PART TWO
HISTORY 11

Chapter 1   Plans and Preparations   12
Chapter 2   The German Defences   20
Chapter 3   The Airborne Assault   40
Chapter 4   The Utah Beach Landings   55
Chapter 5   The D-Day Fighting   69
Chapter 6   Securing the Beachhead   88
Chapter 7   The Capture of Carentan   104

PART THREE
BATTLEFIELD TOURS 111

General Touring Information   112
Tour A   The Merderet Bridgehead   122
Tour B   Sainte-Mère-Église   133
Tour C   The Atlantic Wall   149
Tour D   The Landing Beaches   160
Tour E   The Carentan Causeway   176

PART FOUR
ON YOUR RETURN 185

Further Research   186

Index   189

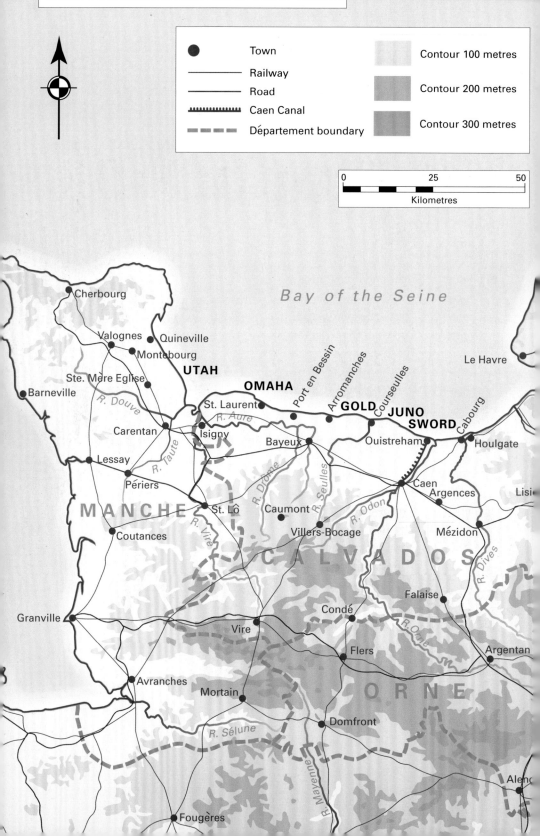

THE NORMANDY BATTLEFIELD

●	Town
————	Railway
————	Road
▬▬▬▬	Caen Canal
▬ ▬ ▬	Département boundary

Contour 100 metres
Contour 200 metres
Contour 300 metres

0   25   50
Kilometres

Bay of the Seine

Cherbourg

Valognes   Quineville
Montebourg
Ste. Mère Eglise   **UTAH**
Barneville   *R. Douve*
St. Laurent   **OMAHA**   Port en Bessin   Arromanches   Courseulles   Le Havre
Carentan   *R. Aure*   **GOLD**   **JUNO**
Isigny   **SWORD**   Cabourg
Lessay   Bayeux   Ouistreham   Houlgate
R. Taute   *R. Drôme*   *R. Seulles*   *R. Odon*   Caen
Périers   Argences
MANCHE   St. Lô   Caumont   Lisi
Coutances   Villers-Bocage   Mézidon
R. Vire   **C A L V A D O S**
R. Dives
Falaise
Granville   Condé   *R. Orne*
Vire   Argentan
Flers
Avranches   **O R N E**
Mortain
Domfront   Alenç
R. Sélune
R. Mayenne
Fougères

PART ONE

INTRODUCTION

BATTLE ZONE NORMANDY

The Battle of Normandy was one of the greatest military clashes of all time. From late 1943, when the Allies appointed their senior commanders and began the air operations that were such a vital preliminary to the invasion, until the end of August 1944, it pitted against one another several of the most powerful nations on earth, as well as some of their most brilliant minds. When it was won, it changed the world forever. The price was high, but for anybody who values the principles of freedom and democracy, it is difficult to conclude that it was one not worth paying.

I first visited Lower Normandy in 1994, a year after I joined the War Studies Department at the Royal Military Academy Sandhurst (RMAS). With the 50th anniversary of D-Day looming, it was decided that the British Army would be represented at several major ceremonies by one of the RMAS's officer cadet companies. It was also suggested that the cadets should visit some of the battlefields, not least to bring home to them the significance of why they were there. Thus, at the start of June 1994, I found myself as one of a small team of military and civilian directing staff flying with the cadets in a draughty and noisy Hercules transport to visit the beaches and fields of Calvados, in my case for the first time.

I was hooked. Having met some of the veterans and seen the ground over which they fought – and where many of their friends died – I was determined to go back. Fortunately, the Army encourages battlefield touring as part of its soldiers' education, and on numerous occasions since 1994 I have been privileged to return to Normandy, often to visit new sites. In the process I have learned a vast amount, both from my colleagues (several of whom are contributors to this series) and from my enthusiastic and sometimes tri-service audiences, whose professional insights and penetrating questions have frequently made me re-examine my own assumptions and prejudices. Perhaps inevitably, especially when standing in one of Normandy's beautifully-maintained Commonwealth War Graves Commission cemeteries, I have also found myself deeply moved by the critical events that took place there in the summer of 1944.

'Battle Zone Normandy' was conceived by Jonathan Falconer, Commissioning Editor at Sutton Publishing, in 2001. Why not, he suggested, bring together recent academic research – some of which challenges the general perception of what happened on and after 6 June 1944 – with a perspective based on familiarity with the ground itself? We agreed that the opportunity existed for a series that would set out to combine detailed and accurate narratives, based mostly on primary sources, with illustrated guides to the ground itself, which could be used either in the field (sometimes quite literally), or by the armchair explorer. The book in your hands is the product of that agreement.

The 'Battle Zone Normandy' series consists of 14 volumes, covering most of the major and many of the minor engagements that went together to create the Battle of Normandy. The first six books deal with the airborne and amphibious landings on 6 June 1944, and with the struggle to create the firm lodgement that was the prerequisite for eventual Allied victory. Five further volumes cover some of the critical battles that followed, as the Allies' plans unravelled and they were forced to improvise a battle very different from that originally intended. Finally, the last three titles in the series examine the fruits of the bitter attritional struggle of June and July 1944, as the Allies irrupted through the German lines or drove them back in fierce fighting. The series ends, logically enough, with the devastation of the German armed forces in the 'Falaise Pocket' in late August.

Whether you use these books while visiting Normandy, or to experience the battlefields vicariously, we hope you will find them as interesting to read as we did to research and write. Far from the inevitable victory that is sometimes represented, D-Day and the ensuing battles were full of hazards and unpredictability. Contrary to the view often expressed, had the invasion failed, it is far from certain that a second attempt could have been mounted. Remember this, and the significance of the contents of this book, not least for your life today, will be the more obvious.

Dr Simon Trew
Royal Military Academy Sandhurst
December 2003

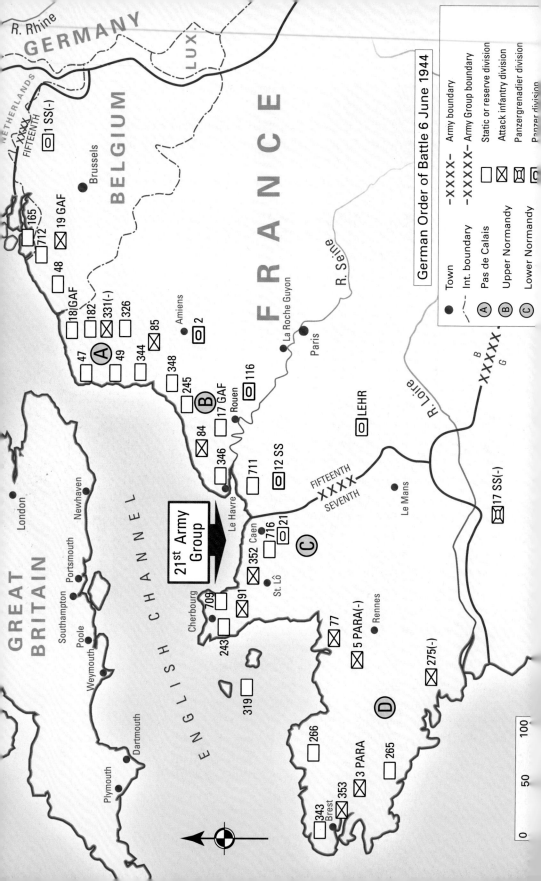

German Order of Battle 6 June 1944

Town •
Int. boundary ---·---·---
Pas de Calais Ⓐ
Upper Normandy Ⓑ
Lower Normandy Ⓒ

Army boundary -XXXX-
Army Group boundary -XXXXX-
Static or reserve division ☐
Attack infantry division ☒
Panzergrenadier division ☒
Panzer division ☒

GERMANY

R. Rhine

NETHERLANDS

LUX.

BELGIUM

Brussels

FRANCE

R. Seine

La Roche Guyon

Paris

R. Loire

XXXX
FIFTEENTH

1 SS(-)

165
712
19 GAF
48
18 GAF
182
331(-)
326
Ⓐ
47
49
344
85
Amiens
2
348
245
Ⓑ
17 GAF
Rouen
116
84
346
711
12 SS
FIFTEENTH
XXXX
SEVENTH
LEHR
Le Mans
17 SS(-)

ENGLISH CHANNEL

GREAT BRITAIN

London
Newhaven
Portsmouth
Southampton
Poole
Weymouth
Dartmouth
Plymouth

Le Havre
Caen
716
21
Ⓒ
352
St. Lô
Cherbourg
709
91
243
319
77
5 PARA(-)
Rennes
275(-)
Ⓓ
266
265
343
Brest
353
3 PARA

21st Army Group

0   50   100

PART TWO

HISTORY

HISTORY

CHAPTER 1

PLANS AND PREPARATIONS

The beach area given the code-name 'Utah Beach' was the westernmost of the five Allied landing beaches on D-Day, Tuesday 6 June 1944, located on the eastern side of the base of the Cotentin peninsula that juts northward out from Lower Normandy into the English Channel. The landing took place from the sea just after dawn on D-Day, led by American troops of the 4th Infantry Division, part of US VII Corps under Major General (Maj Gen) J. Lawton ('Lighting Joe') Collins, and preceded by a night landing by the 82nd 'All American' Airborne Division and the 101st 'Screaming Eagles' Airborne Division by parachute and glider behind German lines to help secure the beachhead. The landing at Utah was a success, with the lowest casualties of any of the Allied beaches on D-Day. Over the next few days the troops of VII Corps staked out a defensible beachhead to the north, west and south in the face of repeated German attempts to drive them back into the sea, linking up with the troops of US V Corps from the adjacent Omaha Beach, and preparing the way for the next phase of the battle, the capture of the major port of Cherbourg at the top of the Cotentin peninsula.

Then and Now
Much of the Utah Beach battlefield has not changed since 1944, including the course of the rivers, the height of the hills, the location of the villages, and the paths of most of the roads. Other aspects of the battlefield have altered: new building has taken place, villages have grown and merged, some have been re-named, new and improved roads have been built, and field boundaries have been removed or changed. This account describes the battlefield as it was in 1944. Major differences from the present day are explained in the section on battlefield tours. Timings are based on British Double Summer Time used by the Allies, two hours ahead of GMT and one hour ahead of local French time.

Above: Part of the memorial of the *Musée du Debarquement* at Utah Beach commemorating the D-Day landings. *(Author)*

Page 11: Troops of 8th Infantry Regiment (some still with life-belts from their landing) wading through the inundations inshore from Utah Beach. *(USNA)*

D-Day (originally set for 5 June but delayed 24 hours because of bad weather) was one of the most famous events of the Second World War, the greatest single combined amphibious and air assault in history, and the start of the liberation of France. German plans to defend against an invasion of France from Britain began in 1942, but they were at first a low priority compared to the fighting on the Eastern Front against the Soviet Union. Even in 1944 the Normandy landings were only possible because the resources and armed forces of Nazi Germany were severely overstretched fighting throughout Europe, and defending against the Anglo-American bombing offensive that devastated Germany, and because the western Allies had won almost total command of the seas and the air.

The German higher command was notoriously badly organised, either through overlapping spheres of authority or lack of co-operation and personal rivalry. From his headquarters in Germany, Adolf Hitler, together with his Armed Forces High Command (OKW) staff, exercised ultimate control over all his forces. In March 1942 *Generalfeldmarschall* (Field Marshal) Gerd von Rundstedt was appointed Commander-in-Chief West with his headquarters (OB West) at Paris, responsible for France,

Belgium and the Netherlands. In November 1943 Field Marshal Erwin Rommel was appointed to oversee the coastal defences, known for propaganda purposes as the 'Atlantic Wall', also taking over Army Group B defending northern France and Belgium in January 1944, under Rundstedt's command but with direct access to Hitler. Under Rommel were two armies: Fifteenth Army defending the Pas de Calais region and Upper Normandy, and Seventh Army commanded by *Generaloberst* (Colonel-General) Friedrich Dollmann defending Lower Normandy and Brittany with its headquarters at Le Mans. Seventh Army included LXXXIV Corps under the one-legged veteran *General der Artillerie* (General of Artillery) Erich Marcks, defending Lower Normandy including the Cotentin, with its headquarters at St-Lô.

German High Command

Oberster Befelshaber der Wehrmacht (Armed Forces Commander-in-Chief): *Adolf Hitler*

Oberkommando der Wehrmacht (OKW) (Armed Forces High Command) Chief of Staff: *Generalfeldmarschall* Wilhelm Keitel

Oberbefelshaber West (OB West) (Commander-in-Chief West):
  Generalfeldmarschall Gerd von Rundstedt
  Luftflotte 3 (Third Air Fleet): *Generalfeldmarschall* Hugo Sperrle
  Marinegruppenkommando West (Naval Group West):
  Admiral Theodore Krancke
  Armeegruppe B (Army Group B): *Generalfeldmarschall* Erwin Rommel
    7. Armee (Seventh Army): *Generaloberst* Friedrich Dollmann

German commanders generally agreed that the most likely Allied invasion route was across the Straits of Dover to Calais, and that to keep themselves supplied after the first landings the Allies must capture a major port quickly. But there were major disputes between Rundstedt and Rommel over strategy, in particular Rommel's firm belief that the best chance to defeat the Allies was at the water's edge on D-Day itself. Rundstedt had also only limited control over the *Waffen-SS* (the Nazi Party's own army), and the forces of the German Navy (*Kriegsmarine*) and Air Force (*Luftwaffe*).

The only warships of Naval Group West able to defend the Cotentin were the 5th and 9th E-boat Flotillas based in Cherbourg, each with seven motor torpedo boats (known as *Schnellboote* – 'fast boats' – to the Germans, and as E-boats – 'enemy boats' – to the Allies), and the Germans relied chiefly on

American soldiers coming ashore on Utah Beach on D-Day. *(USNA)*

sea minefields for naval defence. From April 1944 onwards, Allied bombing raids over northern France had also severely reduced German airpower. By 30 May, Third Air Fleet had only 497 aircraft operational compared to thousands of aircraft at the Allies' disposal in Britain. For deception purposes twice the tonnage of Allied bombs was dropped outside the Normandy area as within it, but repeated air raids delayed and damaged the Atlantic Wall defences in Normandy as well.

The decision to land in Normandy rather than near Calais was made in July 1943 by the Anglo-American staff based in England called COSSAC (Chief of Staff to the Supreme Allied Commander). Allied planning for the liberation of France was code-named Operation 'Overlord', with plans for the actual landing code-named Operation 'Neptune'. The strength of the German defences in Normandy was based on their belief that the Calais area should take priority, but that Cherbourg was the most likely objective should the Allies land in Normandy, and that they might land on both sides of the Cotentin simultaneously to capture the port. The Allies had rejected this idea chiefly because the Germans could bottle up the landing force in the peninsula, and much of the ground in the Cotentin was unsuitable for the airfields they intended to build soon after landing.

At the 'Eureka' conference in Tehran in December 1943, US President Franklin D. Roosevelt and British Prime Minister Winston S. Churchill assured their Soviet ally Marshal Josef Stalin that the landing in France would take place in the following May or June. Soon after, General Dwight D. Eisenhower was appointed as overall commander of SHAEF (Supreme Headquarters Allied Expeditionary Force) to carry out Operation Overlord. The Anglo-American Combined Chiefs of Staff ordered Eisenhower on his appointment: 'You will enter the continent of Europe and, in conjunction with the other United Nations, undertake operations aimed at the heart of Germany and the destruction of her armed forces.'

American paratroopers moving past a churchyard not far from Utah Beach on 8 June. (USNA)

Allied High Command

Supreme Commander Allied Expeditionary Force:
General Dwight D. Eisenhower

Deputy Supreme Commander: Air Chief Marshal Sir Arthur Tedder
Chief of Staff: Lieutenant General Walter Bedell Smith
Commander-in-Chief Allied Naval Expeditionary Force: Adm Sir Bertram Ramsay
Commander Allied Expeditionary Air Force:
   Air Chief Marshal Sir Trafford Leigh-Mallory
Commander 21st Army Group: General Sir Bernard L. Montgomery
   US First Army: Lieutenant General Omar N. Bradley
   Second (British) Army: Lieutenant-General Sir Miles Dempsey

Based in southern England, Eisenhower's SHAEF staff was both multi-national and multi-service, rooted in co-operation. But the individual landing beaches were assigned either to First US Army or Second (British) Army (which included Canadian troops), placed together under General Montgomery, in 21st Army Group. The landing beaches were code-named from west to east Utah and Omaha (the two American beaches) and then Gold, Juno and Sword (the Anglo-Canadian beaches). The landings would be made in daylight to allow firepower to be directed from ships and aircraft onto the Atlantic Wall defences, and would be followed by a swift link-up between the beaches to prevent the Germans isolating and destroying them individually.

The landing at Utah Beach was an addition to the original Allied plan as more forces became available for the landings than COSSAC had expected. Orders for the beach were only issued on 27 March 1944. The addition was a major change, as Utah Beach was more than 25 kilometres (km) from Omaha Beach in a direct line, and more than twice that by road across difficult terrain including the flat flood plain of the multiple river estuary system separating the Cotentin from the rest of Lower Normandy, known as the Vire estuary from its largest river. There was a good chance that the troops at Utah would have to fight on their own for some time before the link-up with Omaha. To make the Utah landings as strong as possible, Lieutenant General (Lt Gen) Bradley insisted on a preliminary assault by 82nd and 101st Airborne Divisions. Such a large airborne landing at night had never been tried before and caused great anxiety. Eisenhower's air commander, Air Chief Marshal Leigh-Mallory, predicted up to 80 per cent losses for the two divisions.

HISTORY

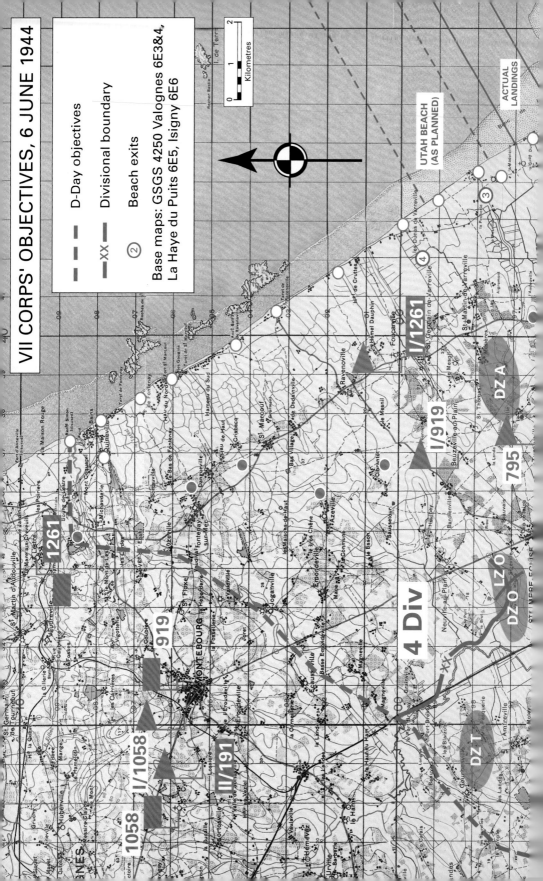

VII CORPS' OBJECTIVES, 6 JUNE 1944

D-Day objectives

xx Divisional boundary

② Beach exits

Base maps: GSGS 4250 Valognes 6E3&4,
La Haye du Puits 6E5, Isigny 6E6

Kilometres
0   1   2

UTAH BEACH
(AS PLANNED)

ACTUAL
LANDINGS

1261

919

1058

I/1058

II/191

4 Div

I/191

I/919

I/1261

795

DZ A

DZ O

LZ O

DZ T

St-Martin-de-Varreville

St-Germain-de-Varreville

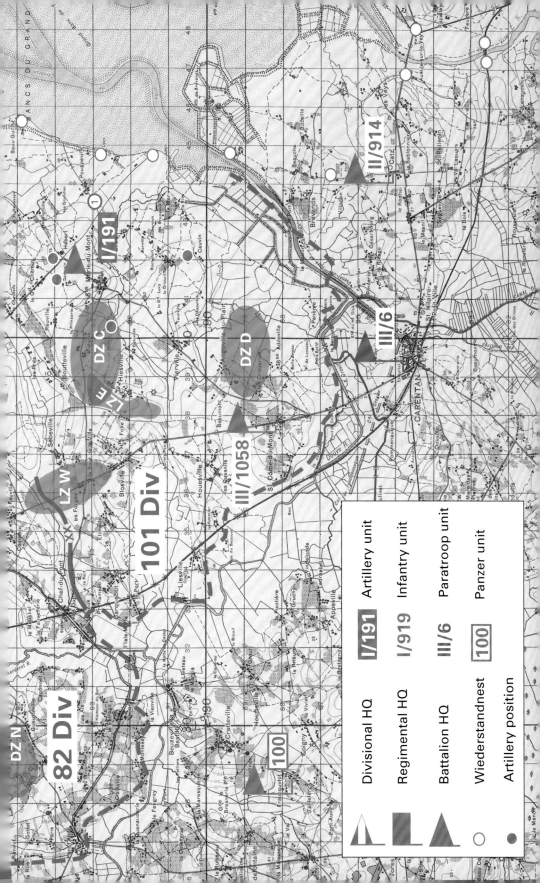

82 Div

DZ N

101 Div

LZ W

DZ C

LZ E

I/191

DZ D

III/1058

II/914

III/6

CARENTAN

100

Divisional HQ	I/191 Artillery unit
Regimental HQ	I/919 Infantry unit
Battalion HQ	III/6 Paratroop unit
Wiederstandnest	100 Panzer unit
Artillery position	

CHAPTER 2

THE GERMAN DEFENCES

The 'Atlantic Wall' proclaimed by German propaganda consisted of beach defences and coastal artillery batteries stretching along the English Channel coast. At this stage of the war the Germans were forced to improvise considerably: formations rarely had a fixed organisation, equipment and weapons came from different countries, good transport was scarce, and many troops and defences were in poor states of preparation and training. In early 1943, 709th Infantry Division was moved to defend the Cotentin peninsula, and in December *Generalmajor* (GenMaj) Karl-Wilhelm von Schlieben was appointed to command it (and was promoted to *Generalleutnant* shortly after), with his headquarters in the château at Saussemesnil 12 km south-east of Cherbourg. This was a 'static division' intended for Atlantic Wall defence, lacking motor transport but strong in artillery, with 12,230 men on 1 May 1944, including many who were above the average age for combat. Three of the division's 11 infantry battalions were *Ost-Bataillonen* ('East-Battalions') recruited in Eastern Europe often from prisoners of war. In the battle most *Ost* battalions surprised Seventh Army by fighting well, but they were not necessarily loyal to the German cause. A high proportion of the

The 'grey' appearance of wet sand on Utah Beach, with the Îles St-Marcouf just visible on the horizon out to sea. *(Author)*

Typical Atlantic Wall defences in 1944, in this case photographed in northern France, showing the various types of fixed obstacles used by the Germans. *(Imperial War Museum CL1)*

division's remaining soldiers were *Volksdeutsche*, German-speaking but not originally from pre-war Germany.

The sector of the Cherbourg defences chosen by the Allies as Utah Beach was a stretch of the south-eastern Cotentin coastline resembling a slightly-straightened fishhook curving to the left. The coastline forming the straight part of the hook was wild and made up of beautiful gold and silver sand beaches (described by the Americans as 'grey' sand) with tall dunes extending inland, stretching from the village of Quinéville and the offshore shoals of the Roches St-Floxel southwards to the estuary of the Rivers Taute and Douve at the Bancs du Grand Vey. The beaches shelved very gently with a gradient of between 1:50 and 1:100, exposing over 700 metres of sand at low tide (high water was between 9.45 and 12.45 twice a day). The coastline had no major landmarks visible from the sea, but two small islands lay offshore where a bank of shallows broke the surface: the Île du Large with a lighthouse and the ruin of a nineteenth century fortress, and the smaller Île de Terre, together forming the Îles St-Marcouf. These were not occupied by the Germans, but were strewn with anti-

Allied Naval Forces at Utah Beach on D-Day

TASK FORCE 122: WESTERN TASK FORCE
Rear Admiral Alan G. Kirk, USN [USS *Augusta*]

Task Force 125: Task Force U
Rear Admiral Don P. Moon, USN, [USS *Bayfield*]
Maj Gen J. Lawton Collins, US Army, VII Corps [also aboard USS *Bayfield*]

Assault Group Green (Tare Green) *Cdr A.L. Warburton, USN* [LCH 530]
(Deputy) *Cdr J.S. Bresman, USCG* [LCI(L) 321]

APA-13 USS *Joseph T. Dickman*
LSI(L) SS *Empire Gauntlet*
US LST Unit: LST 47; LST 48; LST 281
LCC 60 *Lt S.S. Gauthier, USNR*
LCC 70 *Lt S. Freeland, USNR*
US LCI(L) Unit: Division 69 (6 craft); Division 63 (5 craft);
    Division 64 (6 craft); Division 65 (6 craft)
US LCT Unit: Division 19 (6 craft); Division 104 (8 craft);
    Division 22 (6 craft); Division 23 (5 craft); Division 24 (6 craft);
    Division 67 (5 craft); Division 70 (4 craft)
RN LCT units: Flotilla 52 (14 craft); Flotilla 107 (15 craft)
US LCM Unit (26 craft)
LCG (2 craft)
Rhino Ferry Unit (3 craft)

Assault Group Red (Uncle Red) *Cdr E.W. Wilson, USNR* [LCH 10]
(Deputy) *Lt Cdr R.G. Newbegin, USNR* [LCI(L) 217]

APA-33 USS *Bayfield*
APA-5 USS *Barnett*
US LST Unit: LST 282; LST 230
LCC 80 *Lt T. Glennon, USN*
LCC 90 *Lt J.A. White, USN*
US LSI(L) Unit: Division 7 (4 craft); Division 9 (6 craft);
    Division 10 (6 craft); Division 60 (6 craft)
US LCT Unit: Division 20 (6 craft); Division 21 (7 craft);
    Division 99 (7 craft); Division 100 (6 craft); Division 101 (6 craft);
    Division 102 (7 craft)
RN LCT units: Flotilla 44 (5 craft); Flotilla 50 (11 craft);
    Flotilla 104 (7 craft); Flotilla 110 (15 craft)
US LCM Unit (26 craft)
Rhino Ferry Unit (2 craft)

Task Force U Support Group *Lt Cdr L.E. Hart, USNR*
Fire Support Unit 6: 4 x LCG (Large)
Fire Support Unit 7: 5 x LCT (Rocket)
Fire Support Unit 8: 12 x LCS (Small)
Fire Support Unit 9: 4 x LCF
Fire Support Unit 10: 8 x LCT (Armoured)
Fire Support Unit 11: LCP(L) Smoke

BOMBARDMENT FORCE A *Rear Adm M.L. Deyo, USN* [USS *Tuscaloosa*]

(Ships listed by D-Day position north to south and by primary target)

HMS *Erebus* (monitor, 2 x 15-in + 6 x 4-in)	*La Pernelle & Barfleur batteries*
HMS *Black Prince* (cruiser, 5 x 6-in)	*Morsalines battery*
USS *Tuscaloosa* (cruiser, 9 x 8-in + 8 x 5-in)	*Ozeville battery*
USS *Quincy* (cruiser, 9 x 8-in + 12 x 5-in)	*Crisbecq battery*
USS *Nevada* (battleship, 10 x 14-in, 16 x 5-in)	*Azeville battery*
HMS *Enterprise* (cruiser, 5 x 6-in)	*Utah Beach West*
HNMS *Soemba* (sloop, 3 x 5.9-in)	*Utah Beach East*
HMS *Hawkins* (cruiser, 7 x 7.5-in, 4 x 4-in)	*Maisy & St-Martin-de-Varreville batteries*

Destroyers (All US Navy)

Bates; Bunch; Butler; Corry; Fitch; Forrest; Gherardi; Glennon; Herndon; Hobson; Jeffers; Rich; Shubrick

Patrol Craft

PC 484; PC 619; PC 1176; PC 1232; PC 1233; PC 1252; PC 1261; PC 1262; PC 1263

Anti-Submarine Trawlers

HMS *Flint*; HMS *Foulness*; HMS *Texada*

British Minesweepers and Motor Launches

HMSs *Guysborough; Kenora; Poole; Romney; Rye; Seaham; Vegreville; Whitehaven; Beaumaris; Dornoch; Ilfracombe; Parsborough; Qualicum; Shippigan; Tadoussac; Wedgport*

MVs *Blyth; Canso; Commander Evans; Kings Grey; Georgian; Peterhead; Sir Galahad; Sir Lancelot*

Motor Launches 116; 117; 212; 300; 122; 124; 208; 253; 155; 190; 191; 195; 490; 591; 905

Harbour Defence Motor Launches 1295; 1309; 1389; 1409; 1421; 1422

US Minesweepers

Auk; Broadbilt; Chickadee; Nuthatch; Pheasant; Staff; Swift; Threat; Tide; Raven; Osprey

NB: Numerous smaller ships and craft carried out roles for the Western Task Force or for the Allied naval forces generally rather than as part of Task Force U, including salvage vessels, smoke making trawlers, depot and repair ships, ancillary ships etc.

Key: APA Amphibious Transport, LCC Landing Craft Control, LCF Landing Craft Flak, LCG(L) Landing Craft Gun (Large), LCH Landing Craft Headquarters, LCI(L) Landing Craft Infantry (Large), LCM Landing Craft Mechanised, LCP(L) Landing Craft Personnel (Large), LCS Landing Craft Support, LCT Landing Craft Tank, LSI(L) Landing Ship Infantry (Large), LST Landing Ship Tank

Source: [Commander L.J. Pitcairn-Jones, RN], *Operation 'Neptune': The Landings in Normandy 6th June 1944* British Naval Staff History Battle Summary Number 39, 1952 – reprinted London: HMSO, 1994.

personnel mines, and an inshore sea minefield was laid along the shallows. The last ten kilometres of dunes, including la Grande Dune where US VII Corps would land on D-Day, were partly faced by a concrete seawall between two and three metres high. As at other Normandy beaches, British frogmen of the Combined Operations Pilotage Parties made secret landings in 1943, checking that the sand was firm and could take heavy vehicles.

In fact Utah Beach had seen two previous wartime landings, by the Vikings in 841, and by the Royal Navy in 1793 to rescue royalists escaping the French Revolution.

A typical *Stützpunkt* (strongpoint) set slightly inland from Utah Beach. This example is close to les Dunes de Varreville. The coastal ridge on which the German artillery positions were sited is visible in the background. *(Author)*

South of la Grande Dune, the coastline curved round to become marshland, meeting the mouth of the River Taute, part of the Vire estuary system of marshes and flat ground riddled with small rivers and streams; the River Vire itself marked its eastern boundary. Visible across the estuary from Utah Beach were the cliffs of the Pointe du Hoc, the site of a 155-mm coastal battery position that was part of the D-Day objectives for the Omaha Beach landings. Just downstream from the small town of Carentan, the Taute was joined by the River Douve flowing from the west out of the Cotentin. To the south-west of Carentan the ground rose up to a ridge designated Hill 30 (metres), otherwise the area was largely flat marsh or farmland.

Typical farmyard buildings of the Cotentin area near Utah Beach, occupied by American troops on 10 June. *(USNA)*

The Allies divided the Normandy shoreline and sea approaches into code-named segments. At Utah Beach the water inshore of the Îles St-Marcouf was Area Vermont, within which the D-Day landings would take place, the next area directly out to sea was Area Prairie, including the locations for the large warships of Bombardment Force A supporting the Utah Beach landings. Still further out to sea was Area Hickory, including the Transport Area where the landing ships and landing craft of Task Force U were to assemble before commencing the assault.

The coastline at Utah Beach was divided by the Allies into segments southwards from Quinéville using a military phonetic alphabet, and further divided into colours. Lt Gen Bradley's First Army planned for the landing to be made by two battalions side by side, each on a frontage of about 2,000 metres with a gap of 1,000 metres between them, on Tare Green and Uncle Red beaches at 0630 hours, just over 30 minutes after dawn on the

HISTORY

rising tide. The airborne landings would begin about five hours before, giving the paratroopers the time to secure their objectives before dawn. Two of these objectives lay on the River Taute downstream from Carentan. One was the lock at la Barquette (for which the plans had been stolen by the French Resistance and passed to the Allies), at the confluence of the Taute with the Douve. The other was the two wooden bridges (one for vehicles, one for foot traffic; neither bridge exists today) further downriver at le Port, on the opposite shore close to the village of Brévands which was defended by a German strongpoint.

The distinctive church tower at Ste-Marie-du-Mont, taken from the D913 road looking east. *(Author)*

Once past the sand dunes of Utah Beach, the first two or three kilometres directly inland were cattle pasture reclaimed from marshland by drainage ditches or culverts and crossed by multiple tracks. These pastures had been reflooded by the Germans as a precaution well in advance of D-Day (partly by using a sea lock on the estuary coast south of Utah Beach), turning the tracks into causeways through the inundations. These led inland to an uneven ridgeline rising to about 30 metres high that followed the hook-like curve of the coastline and river estuary. A good road ran along the top of this ridge with village settlements on either side of it, starting with Ste-Marie-du-Mont ('Saint Mary on the Hill') in the south. This road was crossed by the smaller roads from the beaches at right angles to form a rough grid pattern. The causeway roads leading from the beaches were given code-names by the Americans: Exit 1 leading to the hamlet of Pouppeville, Exit 2 leading to Ste-Marie-du-Mont, Exit 3 leading to the hamlet of Audouville-la-Hubert, and Exit 4 leading to St-Martin-de-Varreville. The ridge was broken south of Exit 3 by the valley of a small flooded stream.

Exit 1 from Utah Beach towards Pouppeville as it appears today, looking south. *(Author)*

Once away from the marshes, the countryside of the Cotentin was more rugged and hilly than that facing the other Allied beaches, but showed the same settlement pattern of the *bocage* or hedgerow country, the product of centuries of dairy pasturing and apple farming. The *bocage* was a quiltwork of small irregular fields bounded by earth banks topped with dense and deeply-rooted hedgerows and interspersed with orchards, with narrow overgrown dirt roads and tracks running along the field boundaries. Both in the villages and outlying farms, most buildings were medieval in origin with thick stone walls and cellars; and churches had tall spires or towers providing good observation and prominent landmarks. In June the trees were in leaf, and the lush vegetation made this blind country in which movement and fighting were intensely difficult.

The only first class metalled road through the Normandy battlefield was an old Roman road from Caen through Bayeux to Cherbourg. This ran through Carentan north-westerly along a narrow causeway raised above the marshland, briefly in parallel with the railway line to Cherbourg a few hundred metres to the west, and then up onto the ridge at St-Côme-du-Mont and onwards to the north, crossing the gently sloping ridges and valleys to the next small town of Ste-Mère-Église. Further northwards the road ran up onto a considerable ridge extending south-west to le Ham and east to Quinéville on the coast, with Mont Castre just north of the town of Montebourg its highest point at 108 metres. This main Cherbourg road was critical for movement in the region, and Ste-Mère-Église was a major objective in the battle.

A typical farm track through the hedgerow country near Utah Beach. Showing improvements made since 1944, this view was taken just off the D129 road near Hiesville. *(Author)*

Upstream from its confluence with the River Taute just north of Carentan, the River Douve flowed parallel to the main Cherbourg road, gradually turning away westwards. A minor tributary of the Douve, the River Merderet (a name best translated as 'little open sewer'), continued through the water meadows west of Ste-Mère-Église and the Cherbourg railway, with bridges at the village of Chef-du-Pont and at the farmhouse of the Manoir de la Fière, both roads meeting further west at the village of Pont l'Abbé. Neither river was itself a major obstacle, but both frequently flooded the surrounding area in winter. Starting in 1942, the Germans made this flooding permanent (partly by manipulating the sea lock at la Barquette) turning the pastures on either side of both rivers into a swamp sometimes more than waist deep, and the roads at the bridges into easily defended causeways. The owner of la Fière, Monsieur Louis Leroux, recorded that the distance along the flooded causeway was 650 metres from shore to shore. As months passed, much of the inundations became hidden from Allied reconnaissance by green vegetation growing up through the water.

In April 1944, 709th Infantry Division was reinforced by the higher quality 243rd Infantry Division from Brittany, 11,529 strong, sent to defend the western Cotentin. This division was only partly motorised by D-Day, and its 921st Grenadier Regiment (missing its 2nd Battalion) and 922nd Grenadier Regiment were equipped only with bicycles. It was followed in May by 91st Airlanding Division, a division no more than 8,000 strong nominally formed to make glider assaults, held under Seventh Army reserve in the west and central Cotentin. At the same time 6th Paratroop (*Fallschirmjäger*) Regiment moved to the Cotentin. This was a high quality formation more than 3,500 strong. As a reflection of the complexity of the German command structures, 6th Paratroop Regiment was an Air Force unit coming administratively under II Paratroop Corps, but took its tactical orders directly from LXXXIV Corps, and relied on 91st Airlanding Division for its supplies.

The River Merderet at la Fière, looking north from the bridge. In 1944 the open meadow on the left of the picture was entirely under water. *(Author)*

HISTORY

Even after this reinforcement, 709th Infantry Division was widely spread out protecting a front of 110 km, with most of its units located close to Cherbourg. The French civilian population remained in the Cotentin, and German troops performed occupation duties as well as defence against invasion; most towns had a small German garrison. The need to build and strengthen the Atlantic Wall also left little time for training. The German command structure produced many disputes between commanders before and during the battle. What was agreed was that the defences were weaker than opposite the other Allied landing beaches, although the flooded ground itself represented a major obstacle. These disputes continued after the war; and the following reconstruction of the German defences is an attempt to reconcile partial and contradictory records, including eyewitness recollections and testimony.

The view from the top of the ridge at St-Côme-du-Mont south across the plain of the Vire estuary with Carentan in the distance. *(Author)*

On D-Day the battalion of 709th Infantry Division responsible for the Utah Beach coastline from Quinéville southward was 1st Battalion, 919th Hessian-Thüringian Grenadier Regiment (I/919th Grenadiers), with its battalion headquarters near Foucarville and one company held in local reserve at Ste-Marie-du-Mont. The coast to the north was held by II/919th Grenadiers, and III/919th Grenadiers were in divisional reserve north-west of Quinéville, together with a battalion of 729th

German Order of Battle

LXXXIV CORPS *General der Artillerie Erich Marcks*

91st Airlanding Division *(91. Luftlande-Division)*
Generalleutnant Wilhelm Falley
1057th Grenadier Regt, 1058th Grenadier Regt,
191st Artillery Regt, 191st Assault Gun Company, 191st Flak Company,
191st Engineer Battalion, 91st Fusilier Battalion

243rd Infantry Division *(243. Infanterie-Division)*
Generalleutnant Heinz Hellmich
920th Grenadier Regt, 921st Grenadier Regt, 922nd Grenadier Regt,
243rd Artillery Regt, 243rd Anti-Tank Battalion, 243rd Engineer Battalion

709th Infantry Division *(709. Infanterie-Division)*
Generalleutnant Karl-Wilhelm von Schlieben
729th Grenadier Regt, 739th Grenadier Regt, 919th Grenadier Regt,
1709th Artillery Regt, 709th Anti-Tank Battalion, 709th Engineer Battalion

6th Paratroop Regt *(Fallschirmjäger-Regiment 6)*
Major Friedrich-August von der Heydte
1st Paratroop Battalion, 2nd Paratroop Battalion, 3rd Paratroop Battalion,
Heavy Mortar Company, Anti-Tank Company, Engineer Company

Seventh Army Assault Battalion *(Sturm-Bataillon AOK 7)*

100th Panzer Training and Replacement Battalion
(Panzer-Ausbildungs-und-Ersatz-Abteilung 100)

206th Panzer Battalion *(Panzer-Abteilung 206)*

Grenadiers and 709th Anti-Tank Battalion. Just inland from Utah Beach, deployed from the crossroads between Exit 3 and the coastal ridge road inland to the main Cherbourg road, was an *Ost* battalion from the Soviet Union, 795th Georgian Battalion, detached from 739th Grenadier Regiment and lacking one company. The divisional boundary to the south ran along the River Taute. The Vire estuary area was defended by 914th Grenadiers, part of the stronger 352nd Infantry Division which fought mainly against US V Corps on Omaha Beach on D-Day.

The Atlantic Wall in the Utah Beach sector was based on concrete bunker positions called *Wiederstandnester* ('resistance nests') or *Stützpunkte* ('strongpoints') built into the sand dunes and along the seawall. Before D-Day, Allied Intelligence identified 18 resistance nests and strongpoints along Utah Beach from Quinéville to Brévands. At Utah these were numbered consecutively from the south, and sited to cover the exit roads from the beach. At least two numbering systems were used, with some German maps showing what US sources refer to as WN-1

GERMAN DEFENCES ON UTAH BEACH

NOTES
1. Most positions were wired in and at least partly surrounded by real and/or dummy minefields.
2. Armament in main table refers to larger guns only. Most positions also included mortars, machine guns and other weapons for local defence.
3. Positions of 3 further companies of 3rd Battalion, 1058th Grenadier Regiment near St-Côme-du-Mont and Ste-Marie-du-Mont are unknown.
4. Various flak, supply, signal and headquarters elements not shown (eg. flak supply unit at Ste-Mère-Église).
5. Sources are contradictory and incomplete regarding German artillery positions. The map represents our best attempt to address these difficulties, but may contain minor errors.

Base maps: GSGS 4250 Valognes 6E3&4, Isigny 6E6, La Haye du Puits 6E5

① WN-92 Armament unknown
② WN-99 Armament unknown
③ WN-100 ('WN-1') 1 x 75-mm, 2 x 50-mm, 1 x 37-mm
④ WN-101 ('WN-2') Local defence
⑤ WN-102 ('WN-3') 1 x 50-mm; 1 x 47-mm
⑥ WN-103 ('WN-4') Local defence
⑦ WN-104 ('WN-5') 1 x 88-mm, 2 x 75-mm, 1 x 50-mm
⑧ WN-105 ('WN-6') Local defence
⑨ WN-106 ('WN-7') 2 x 50-mm, 1 x 47-mm, 1 field piece
⑩ WN-100 2 x 88-mm; 1 x 37-mm
⑪ WN-101 1 x 88-mm, 2 x 50-mm, 2 x 47-mm, 2 x 37-mm
⑫ WN-102 1 x 50-mm; 2 x 37-mm
⑬ WN-103 1 x 88-mm, 1 x 50-mm, 2 x 37-mm
⑭ WN-104 2 x 50-mm
⑮ WN-104a 2 x 88-mm; 4 x 37-mm
⑯ Field position 6 x 155-mm (3/1261)
⑰ S-135 4 x 210-mm; 1 x 150-mm (naval battery)
⑱ S-134 6 x 75-mm flak; 3 x 20-mm flak
⑲ S-133 4 x 105-mm; 2 x 37-mm flak (2/1261)
⑳ Field position 4 x 100-mm (7th Assault Battalion)
   3 x 122-mm (1/1261) in unidentified position nearby
㉑ WN-108 Position abandoned before D-Day
㉒ Field position 4 x 105-mm (191st Artillery Regiment)
㉓ WN-110 4 x 76.2-mm (elements 13/919)
㉔ Field position 4 x 105-mm (191st Artillery Regiment)
㉕ Field position 4 x 105-mm (191st Artillery Regiment)
㉖ Field position 2 x 76.2-mm (elements 13/919)

- XX -   Divisional boundary

▶   Battalion HQ

1/1261   Artillery battery

3/919   Infantry company

19

4/919

I/1261

Coy 795

3/919

Coy 795

2/919

I/191

1/919

Coy 1058

709 Div

352 Div

4/914

A typical German gun position at Utah Beach: a 50-mm anti-tank gun in a concrete emplacement, located opposite Foucarville village just north of the American landing area. Equally typical beach defences are visible on the sands in the background. Photograph taken on 14 June. *(USNA)*

as WN-100. WN-5 (also known as WN-104) defended Exit 2 at la Grande Dune, with a strongpoint just inland near the little hamlet and chapel of la Madeleine, and another resistance nest defending Exit 3. (To increase the potential for confusion, some German maps identified a second series of positions beginning at WN-100 on the coast east of St-Martin-de-Varaville; US sources again identify these differently.)

The Germans expected the Allies to land close to high tide (possibly at night), and the beaches were covered with wooden, concrete and steel obstacles intended to be submerged just below the surface when the tide was high. The Allied decision to land on a rising tide meant that the landing craft touched down in waist or chest-high water about 300 metres in front of the exposed obstacles, which extended for a further 400 metres inland to the high water mark, with the seawall and the 5-metre high sand dunes less than 20 metres beyond.

The beach defences at WN-5/WN-104 (later documented by US Engineers) were typical of the Atlantic Wall, although weaker than other resistance nests further north along the beach. From the sea inshore, first came eight 'Belgian Gates' or Type 3 obstacles, a metal latticework about three metres square also used as a roadblock; then some scattered wooden or curved metal ramps four metres long each supported by a bipod and facing inshore for the flat-bottomed landing craft to ride up and capsize. Then came three rows of concrete posts and pyramids about two metres high, some rows separate and some mixed together, set about ten metres apart with fifteen metres between the rows. The final obstacle consisted of a similar three rows of thick wooden posts up to two metres high, in some places reaching up to the seawall and in others stopping up to 200 metres short (although not topped with mines, as was otherwise a common German practice). The wall itself was ramped with sand in several places on its seaward side, and topped by a barbed wire fence. At Utah the strong currents and shelving sands meant that many obstacles washed away at high tide, and the beach defences needed constant repair.

Both the sand dunes and seawall, and the exits to the causeway roads defended by the resistance nests, were mined, wired, and blocked by obstacles including anti-tank ditches, metal girders welded into caltrops or 'hedgehogs', and wheeled versions of the Belgian Gate. The resistance nests at Utah all conformed to a common pattern, consisting of the seawall as an anti-tank obstacle, an underground command post, and machine guns, automatic flame throwers, and anti-tank guns, both in open emplacements and in concrete bunkers or casemates set to enfilade the beach. WN-5/WN-104 covered about 400 by 300 metres, and was manned by part of 3rd Company, I/919th Grenadiers, under *Leutnant* (2nd Lieutenant) Arthur Jahnke, a 23-year-old veteran with the Knight's Cross who had been seriously wounded on the Eastern Front. Facing out to sea it had a central 'Tobruk pit' (a concrete emplacement named after the Libyan port, scene of heavy fighting in 1941–42) fitted with a machine gun in a turret taken from a French Renault FT17 tank. According to Jahnke's disputed account this was flanked by an 88-mm gun and two automatic flame throwers, supported by two 50-mm and two 75-mm regimental anti-tank guns and an 80-mm mortar in a pit, plus eight 'Goliath' miniature tracked demolition vehicles each packed with 100 kilograms of explosives. Known to the Americans as 'Doodlebugs', these were steered by radio control up to an enemy vehicle and then exploded.

Rommel's emphasis on stopping the Allies on the beaches meant that there was little time or material left for roadblocks or

Simple obstacles made from wooden posts on Utah Beach, north of the first landing sites. These posts were covered with water at high tide. The post in the foreground has an anti-tank mine strapped to its top, a not uncommon practice. Photographed on 15 September. *(USNA)*

further defences inland. Possible Allied airborne landing sites were identified and nearby buildings prepared for defence or for setting on fire to provide illumination at night. From May onwards, tall poles were erected in the larger fields as a defence against gliders, known to the German troops as 'Rommel's Asparagus' (*Rommelsspargel*), with a planned completion date of 15 June.

The beach defences and inundations were backed by artillery batteries along the coastal ridge covering the beaches and their exits. Responsibility for the eastern Cotentin coastline lay with 1261st Army Coastal Artillery Regiment (1261st Coastal Artillery), then further north as far as the north-west headland with 1709th Artillery Regiment (709th Infantry Division's artillery), then 1262nd Coastal Artillery defending the western coastline (but with some long-range guns capable of moving to shell the eastern beaches). Some artillery batteries defending Utah Beach were mobile, protected by earth and wood trenches or concrete bunkers but with alternate locations; others were fixed in concrete casemates. Including the long-range batteries such as the Pointe du Hoc, Allied Intelligence identified 28 German batteries with 111 medium and heavy guns capable of shelling the forces landing on Utah Beach, and estimated that at least three-quarters of these guns were still operational on D-Day, despite repeated air attacks.

A low aerial view of one of the 210-mm gun casemates of the Crisbecq battery, photographed on 8 July after its capture. Part of the battery command post is just visible on the far side of the dirt road. *(USNA)*

In the immediate landing area, the Allies identified ten German battery positions from Quinéville southwards, probably including dummy or alternate sites. The headquarters of 1261st Coastal Artillery and a casemated battery crewed by the German Navy occupied the high ground inland just north-west of Quinéville called 'Ginster Hill' by the Germans, with elements of 4th Battery, 1261st Coastal Artillery, (4/1261st) at Quinéville itself. The most powerful battery defending Utah was at Crisbecq with four 210-mm Skoda guns, two in casemates, also crewed by the Navy and linked to 2/1261st Coastal Artillery nearby at Azeville which had four 105-mm Schneider guns in casemates.

These were (from north to south) 3/1261st Coastal Artillery battery with six 155-mm guns at Fontenay-sur-Mer; then 1/1261st Coastal Artillery with three Russian-made 122-mm guns near Cibrantot (these had been at St-Martin-de-Varaville until shortly before D-Day); then I/191st Artillery Regiment (from 91st Airlanding Division) with three batteries each of four

View from the command post of the Crisbecq battery, looking eastward through the hedgerows towards the beach along what is now the D69 road leading to les Gauguins. The gun casemate position is out of shot to the left. *(Author)*

105-mm guns around Ste-Marie-du-Mont, with the battalion headquarters in the village. Many of these sites had been heavily bombed before D-Day, notably the position at St-Martin-de-Varaville, which was abandoned (along with one of its 122-mm guns) because of these attacks. Also on the ridge close to Ste-Marie-du-Mont near the crossroads with Exit 2 were a battery of *Nebelwerfer* multi-barrelled rocket launchers and four Russian 76.2-mm howitzers of 919th Grenadiers' infantry gun company (two more guns were south of the village covering the River Taute), and nearby a platoon of the regiment's anti-tank company with three 75-mm guns. More anti-tank guns, from 1058th Grenadier Regiment's anti-tank company (also 91st Airlanding Division) were stationed 5 km west of Ste-Marie-du-Mont.

These locations could vary, and in another reflection of German command problems not even the German higher commanders were always certain of where the batteries in their area were sited. The detached gun company from Seventh Army Assault Battalion (7th Assault Battalion), a Seventh Army reserve formation created from its training schools, with four light French or Russian howitzers, was believed by GenLt von Schlieben to be dug in near Ste-Marie-du-Mont, but was reported after the battle as sited considerably further north on the ridge at Cibrantot between Foucarville and Azeville.

To defend the main Cherbourg road and support 709th Infantry Division, 1058th Grenadier Regiment was detached from 91st Airlanding Division. Its 3rd Battalion (III/1058th Grenadiers) was located at St-Côme-du-Mont, and the two remaining battalions north of Montebourg. The only reserve armour was 100th Panzer Training and Replacement Battalion (100th Panzer T/R Battalion) with 30 tanks, attached to 91st Airlanding Division north-west of Carentan. Except for one Panzer III these were obsolescent French tanks mostly equipped with 37-mm guns known jokingly as 'tank knockers' from their lack of penetrative power. Further away in the western Cotentin was 206th Panzer Battalion with Russian, French, and Czech light tanks. As a response unit for any Allied parachute landings, 6th Paratroop Regiment was spread out across the base of the Cotentin, with II/6th Paratroop Regiment guarding the sector

A commandeered French tank turret mounted on a Tobruk pit concrete emplacement as part of the Utah Beach defences. Photographed on 15 September. (USNA)

around Lessay, I/6th Paratroop Regiment north of regimental headquarters at Périers, and III/6th Paratroop Regiment located south of Carentan.

CHAPTER 3

THE AIRBORNE ASSAULT

The discovery by Allied Intelligence that 91st Airlanding Division together with 6th Paratroop Regiment had moved into the Cotentin led on 27 May to a late change in the plan for the airborne landings at Utah. The drop area and objectives for the 101st Airborne remained largely unaffected. Troops of the division were to land in three areas; Drop Zone A (DZ A) in the fields west of St-Martin-de-Varreville to secure Exit 4 and Exit 3 from Utah Beach, DZ C to the west of Ste-Marie-du-Mont to secure Exit 2 and Exit 1, and DZ D just east of St-Côme-du-Mont to secure la Barquette lock and the bridges at le Port near Brévands. About 2,000 men from 101st Airborne Division were given training in amphibious landing procedures in order to ease co-operation with 4th Infantry Division. The mission for 82nd Airborne Division was scaled back, from the original plan to seize objectives far to the west, to securing Ste-Mère-Église and a bridgehead across the River Merderet including the crossings at la Fière and Chef-du-Pont. Because of the cramped nature of the hedgerow country, drop zones were selected on either side of the Merderet: DZ O was immediately to the north-west of Ste-Mère-Église, with DZ T to its west and DZ N just north of the la Fière road, both on the western side of the river. All the drop zones for both divisions were perilously close to the inundations either inland from Utah Beach or on either side of the Merderet and Douve. The change of plan also left the western Cotentin free for the Germans to move their reserves after the landings.

Field Order 1 for Operation Overlord issued on 28 May read simply, 'VII Corps assaults Utah beach on D-Day at H-Hour and captures Cherbourg with minimum delay.' The VII Corps' D-Day objectives (including those for 82nd and 101st Airborne, which came under VII Corps once on the ground) included the high ground at St-Côme-du-Mont and bridges to the south, the line of the Douve and the Merderet up to Chef-du-Pont and westward as far as Pont l'Abbé, then ground north-west to the line of the Merderet and across the main Cherbourg road just south of the le Ham–Montebourg–Quinéville ridge to the coast at Quinéville. If D-Day went well, once 4th Infantry Division was fully ashore, 101st Airborne would move south-east to capture Carentan and secure the junction with V Corps from Omaha Beach, which would take place on D-Day or shortly afterwards. On D+1 (7 June) the remaining forces of 82nd and 101st Airborne would arrive at Utah, together with 90th Infantry Division (the 'Tough Ombres' from their linked 'TO' symbol; the division had originally come from Texas and Oregon), followed on D+4 by 9th Infantry Division, and on D+8 by 79th Infantry Division.

Task Force U, the assault and landing forces for Utah Beach, was under the command of Rear Admiral Don P. Moon from his command ship, the Attack Transport Ship APA-33 USS *Bayfield*. The first ships to leave harbour in southern England for

Order of Battle, US Airborne Forces

US Army Air Force Ninth Air Force *Lt Gen Lewis H. Brereton*

IX Troop Carrier Command *Maj Gen Paul Williams*
50th Troop Carrier Wing
439th, 440th, 441st Troop Carrier Groups
52nd Troop Carrier Wing
61st, 313th, 314th, 315th, 316th, 442nd Troop Carrier Groups
53rd Troop Carrier Wing
434th, 435th, 436th, 437th, 438th Troop Carrier Groups

82nd ('All American') Airborne Division
Maj Gen Matthew B. Ridgway
Assistant Commander: *Brig Gen James M. Gavin*

505th PIR, 507th PIR, 508th PIR, 325th GIR [including 2/401st GIR]
456th PFA Battalion, 319th GFA Battalion, 320th GFA Battalion
80th Airborne AAA Battalion (anti-tank), 307th Airborne Engineer Battalion

101st ('Screaming Eagles') Airborne Division
Maj Gen Maxwell D. Taylor
Assistant Commander: *Brig Gen Donald F. Pratt*

501st PIR, 502nd PIR, 506th PIR, 327th GIR [including 1/401st GIR]
321st GFA Battalion, 907th PFA Battalion, 377th PFA Battalion
81st Airborne AAA Battalion, 326th Airborne Engineer Battalion

Key: AAA Anti-Aircraft Artillery, GFA Glider Field Artillery, GIR Glider Infantry Regiment, PFA Parachute Field Artillery, PIR Parachute Infantry Regiment.

Operation Neptune were minesweepers to clear channels for the assault. The slower vessels of Task Force U from Plymouth, and those warships stationed in Belfast harbour with the furthest to travel, began to sail on 3 June, before the order to delay D-Day until 6 June was given. Some of the Utah convoys had to remain at sea through the bad weather, including the Landing Craft Tank (LCTs) and other flat-bottomed craft. By the time the troops landed on the morning of 6 June they had been on a rough sea for three nights and two days, and were utterly seasick. In total Task Force U numbered 865 vessels in twelve separate convoys, merging in mid-Channel before turning for Utah Beach.

On the late afternoon of 5 June, General Eisenhower visited some troops of 101st Airborne at their take-off airfields, including 2nd Battalion, 502nd Parachute Infantry Regiment (2/502nd PIR), at Greenham Common and 3/501st PIR at

A censored photograph of General Eisenhower addressing men of 502nd Parachute Infantry Regiment, 101st Airborne Division, at RAF Greenham Common airfield on 5 June. *(Imperial War Museum EA 25491)*

HISTORY

Welford, before returning at 2100 hours to his headquarters. At 2215 the first 18 C-47 aircraft (the military version of the DC-3 Dakota, with no weapons, armour, or self-sealing fuel tanks) of the USAAF's IX Troop Carrier Command Pathfinder Group began to take off, carrying the divisional pathfinders. They were followed by the start of the main force of aircraft, 432 C-47s of 50th and 53rd Troop Carrier Wings from seven airfields carrying 6,600 paratroopers of 101st Airborne Division, with the first aircraft taking off at 2230 hours, getting into formation, and departing for the Cotentin at 2345. Next came 389 C-47s of 52nd Troop Carrier Wing carrying 6,396 paratroopers of 82nd Airborne Division, the first taking off at 2300 hours. After assembling in formation, the flight to the drop zones took the aircraft on average 58 minutes. The C-47s flew in arrow-head formations of nine aircraft, over the English Channel at 500 feet (170 metres) on a course taking them out to the west before turning just north of the Channel Islands, climbing to 1,500 feet and flying back across the Cotentin from west to east.

The night was brightly moonlit, but with heavy low cloud and rain over Normandy. Some Allied bombing of the landing areas began at about 2230 hours. GenLt von Schlieben and GenLt Falley, commanding 91st Airlanding Division, had set out that night to drive to Rennes for a high-level 'wargame' (a training exercise) due to start at 1000 hours the next day. General Marcks, the LXXXIV Corps commander, remained at his headquarters, intending to travel in the morning. Shortly after 2300 hours on 5 June, Seventh Army went on alert in response to coded radio messages for the French Resistance sent through the BBC. At Ste-Mère-Église, defended by a small contingent from 919th Grenadiers and about 200 Flak troops (anti-aircraft, but with no artillery pieces; the men were responsible for ammunition resupply), the bombing set fire to a large building at a corner of the main square shortly before midnight. The town mayor, Alexandre Renaud, helped organise a chain of fire-fighters using water from the pump near the church, and both German soldiers and French civilians were awake and alert when the paratroopers arrived.

Conflicting claims have been made for the first Allied paratrooper to land in France on D-Day (by French time the first landings took place just after 2300 hours on 5 June). Lieutenant Noel Poole of the British Army's Special Air Service led a three-

The town square pump at Ste-Mère-Église today, with the church in the background. *(Author)*

man team that jumped at 0012 hours, 6 June (Allied time), from an RAF Short Stirling and landed near St-Lô, to take part in the deception and sabotage operations for the invasion. Measures to fool the Germans about the extent of the airborne drop included simulated gunfire, and dummy parachutists made of sacking with firecrackers attached dropped from aircraft across Normandy. French Resistance teams also joined in the deception measures, and in cutting telephone wires to hamper communications. Shortly afterwards, the C-47s with six teams of pathfinders, three from each division, arrived half an hour before the main waves of aircraft, intending to mark the drop zones with 'Eureka' radar beacons and with lights forming a 'T' shape for the landing. Captain Frank L. Lillyman, leading the pathfinders of 101st Airborne, jumped aiming for DZ A at 0015 hours from a C-47 flown by Lieutenant Colonel (Lt Col) Joel Crouch, simultaneously with the first British glider landings near Caen.

Dropping a handful of men by night into hostile territory with the enemy forces on high alert carried great risks. Few of the pathfinders landed where intended, and none of 101st Airborne's drop zones could be correctly marked. Instead, lights and radar beacons were set 1,500 metres north of DZ A, a single light and radar beacon were set 400 metres south-east of DZ C, and a single radar beacon set 1,500 metres west of DZ D, which was under enemy fire. The pathfinders of 82nd Airborne, arriving at 0125 hours, had similar troubles, coming under fire from patrols of 1057th Grenadiers to the west. When the main waves of 82nd Airborne arrived only DZ O was adequately marked, at DZ T no lights and only two beacons were working, and at DZ N the pathfinders were able to set up one beacon and two lights.

The first of the main parachute drops by 101st Airborne began at 0119 hours, with about ten minutes between serials, each regiment taking between ten and fifteen minutes to land. As the C-47s crossed the coast they began to hit low cloud and fog banks over the Cotentin all the way to the line of the Merderct where the fog was thickest. Most of the C-47s were in the fog for

Paratroopers of 82nd Airborne Division making last minute checks of their equipment at RAF Saltby airfield on 5 June. (USNA)

at least five minutes, flying on instruments. To avoid mid-air collision the pilots loosened or broke formation, and some also lost direction. As the aircraft approached their drop zones they began to search for the lights and radar beacons from the pathfinders on the ground. The C-47s came out of the fog over the Merderet and into the flak coming up from the ground; some paratroopers later claimed also to have been fired upon by passing German aircraft. The pilots tried to hold their courses for

HISTORY

the last few seconds, some even circling to get a better drop. At least 21 aircraft were lost and 196 damaged. Every group of the three USAAF Troop Carrier Wings received a Unit Citation for Normandy. Even so, jumps that should have taken place at 700 feet (215 metres) and 110 mph (180 km/hr) were made when many aircraft were outside those limits or well off course when the signal was given. The decision on exactly when to jump was made by the lead paratrooper in each 'stick' (a planeload of between 15 and 18 paratroopers and equipment). As they jumped, paratroopers had equipment torn off by the airstream, were stunned by jump shock as their parachutes opened, or had hard landings after only seconds. Several sticks were dropped over 30 km from their intended drop zones. Many paratroopers came down in the floods of the Merderet or the coastal inundations. An unknown number drowned, and about 60 per cent of all equipment was lost.

The 101st Airborne Division's plan called for all three battalions of 502nd PIR and 377th Parachute Field Artillery Battalion to land in DZ A, 1/506th and 2/506th PIR and 3/501st PIR plus the divisional headquarters to land in DZ C, and 1/501st PIR, 2/501st PIR and 3/506th PIR with 326th Airborne Engineer Battalion to land in DZ D. Almost all the division's troops did land east of the main Cherbourg road, but only 2,500 men landed on their intended drop zones or within reach of other formations. Not a single stick landed on DZ A; most of the troops came down further south, within 4 km of Ste-Marie-du-Mont. A few paratroopers dropped onto German positions in towns or villages, including Ste-Mère-Église. The best drops took place at DZ D near la Barquette lock where 45 planeloads landed on or close to their target. But this had been identified by the Germans as a potential landing site, and came at once under heavy fire illuminated by burning buildings. Maj Gen Taylor, commanding the division, landed safely on DZ C; this was his fifth parachute jump and thus qualified him for his parachute wings as he had not been through jump school.

The 82nd Airborne Division's aircraft arrived between 0200 and 0245 hours. The plan was for 505th PIR to land in DZ O and capture Ste-Mère-Église and the bridges at la Fière and Chef-du-Pont, while 507th PIR landed in DZ T to take positions to the west, and 508th PIR plus divisional headquarters landed in DZ N and moved south-west to set up a defensive line along the River

Private Clarence C. Ware of 506th Parachute Infantry Regiment, 101st Airborne Division, adds to the 'warpaint' worn by Private Charles R. Plaudo on 5 June 1944. This 'Mohican' style of haircut and camouflage paint was adopted by some American paratroopers, to the alarm of French civilians who first encountered them. Private Ware was injured while serving with the regimental demolition team on D-Day. *(USNA)*

Douve. The assistant divisional commander, Brig Gen James Gavin (known as 'Slim Jim' or 'Jumping Jim'), led the division into battle by jumping from the lead aircraft; the slipstream as he jumped tore his watch from his wrist. All but two sticks missed DZ T altogether, and only six landed on DZ N. Most of 507th PIR were dropped into the swamps of the Merderet, and 508th PIR was scattered over a wide area. About 30 paratroopers came down in the middle of Ste-Mère-Église including the main square, where they were killed or captured by the defenders from the Flak unit. At least nine planeloads (plus two from the

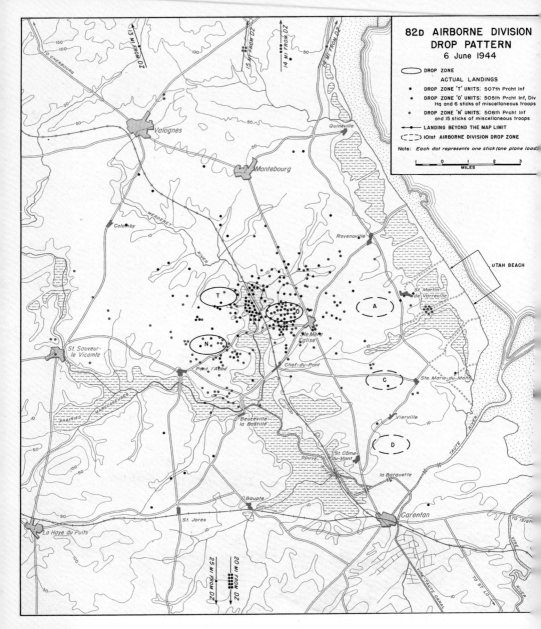

These airborne drop diagrams are taken from the first volume of the US Official History of the Normandy battle, *Cross Channel Attack*. Each dot denotes a 'stick' or planeload of paratroopers, usually of between 15 and 18 men with their equipment. In fact, the dots represent each of the stick leaders' approximate landing points. As can be appreciated, since the C-47s dropping the parachutists were travelling at around 160 km/h (100 mph), the men in each stick would find themselves spread out over at least a kilometre, and possibly over several. The spread would be increased if a nervous pilot flew too fast, as was sometimes the case. The haphazard results, while disorientating for the parachutists themselves, greatly confused the German defenders and considerably amplified the impact of the airborne operations.

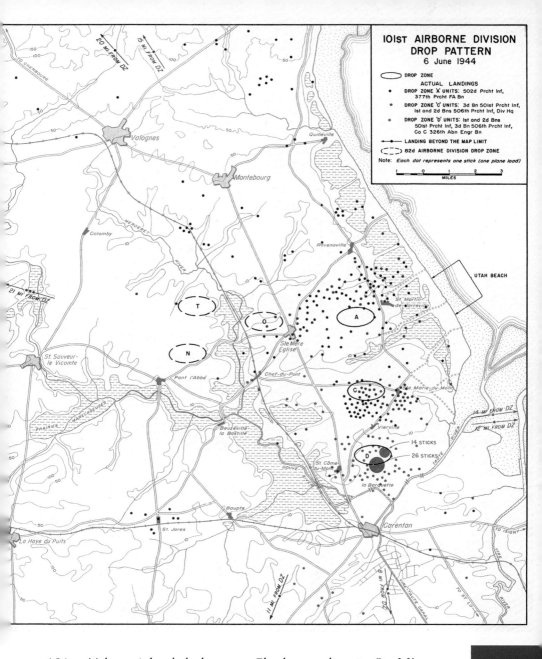

101st Airborne) landed closer to Cherbourg than to Ste-Mère-Église. Most of the sticks landed west of the main Cherbourg road as intended, although 13 sticks came down in 101st Airborne's area, either in the flooding at Exit 3 or close to St-Martin-de-Varreville. Only 505th PIR, which arrived first, had a good drop due in part to some C-47s circling through the flak to get a better approach, with about 1,000 out of 2,500 men of the regiment landing in or close to DZ O, together with Maj Gen Ridgway and his staff.

The interior of a C-47 Skytrain, with a jump master and crew chief pushing parapacks of supplies out of the jump door. Photographed on 7 June. *(USNA)*

Many men of both airborne divisions who survived the drop found themselves scattered throughout the Cotentin in darkness, cut off from their units. Almost without exception, commanding officers had no idea of where they had landed. Many in the 82nd Airborne who had seen light glinting off the water of the inundations seconds before they jumped assumed wrongly that they must have flown over the Merderet or Douve and landed to the east. Once on the ground, the swollen Merderet was also mistaken for the larger Douve. The commanders of 1/501st PIR, 2/501st PIR and 3/506th PIR were killed in the landings; the commander of 502nd PIR suffered a leg injury, as did the commanders of 2/502nd PIR and 2/505th PIR, although both these men remained mobile enough to command their battalions. Most of 3/507th PIR headquarters landed several kilometres south of Carentan. Only one out of six 75-mm howitzers of

377th Parachute Field Artillery was retrieved, and their crews fought for the next few days as infantry. Five battalions – 2/502nd PIR of 101st Airborne, and 1/507th PIR, 3/507th PIR, 1/508th PIR and 3/508th PIR of 82nd Airborne – were so badly scattered that they took no part as formed units on D-Day.

Through the swamps and hedgerows at night, disorientated and often close to exhaustion after the rigours of the flight and airborne descent, and the struggles to rescue themselves from drowing in the floods, small groups assembled and moved towards their objectives like drops of water running together, many moving downslope towards the Merderet and the Cherbourg railway line. In the dark, some men identified friendly soldiers by signalling with the 'cricket' clicking toy they had been given just before departure, others used spoken passwords, or relied on silence and compasses. In many cases, the paratroopers attached themselves to any formation (508th PIR formed into four main groups including men of both divisions), or simply attacked the nearest German position that they could find.

The scattering raised almost as many problems for the Germans as for the Americans, as paratroopers seemed to appear from anywhere. Within LXXXIV Corps, 352nd Infantry Division to the east went onto high alert at 0130 hours and soon afterwards the division reported paratroopers in the Vire estuary, (six planeloads mis-dropped far away from their intended zones). By 0250 reports were coming in of parachute landings all over the Cotentin, including claims of landings on the west coast. At least 30 planeloads were dropped south and west of Carentan into the areas defended by I/6th Paratroop Regiment and III/6th Paratroop Regiment. Some sticks landed near the detached battery from 7th Assault Battalion, which was forced to fight as infantry and was destroyed over the next 48 hours without ever firing its guns. At 0200 hours 795th Georgian Battalion reported itself surrounded by parachutists, and by 0330 91st Airlanding Division also reported that it had lost contact with the troops in the Ste-Mère-Église sector.

Throughout the Cotentin and beyond, German troops were being engaged by Americans emerging out of the dark, and patrols were sent out to hunt down the invaders. It was the kind of fighting at which the highly trained and motivated American paratroopers excelled, and if movement was painfully slow and difficult in the swamps and hedgerows, the ground was perfect

for ambushes. As GenLt Falley returned from Rennes, driving through the night to his headquarters in the château at Haut (north of Picauville and close to Pont l'Abbé), a group of paratroops led by Captain Malcolm Brannen of 3/508th PIR ambushed his car, killing Falley and a staff officer. A regimental commander took temporary control, but Falley's replacement *Oberst* (Colonel) Eugen König did not reach the division until 10 June. GenLt von Schlieben of 709th Infantry Division learnt about the invasion at 0630 hours in Rennes, and was not back at his headquarters until noon. In consequence, two of the three German divisions defending the Cotentin were without their commanders for most of D-Day. Rommel was also absent,

A typical château of the Cotentin area near Utah Beach, occupied by US airborne troops on D-Day or shortly afterwards. *(USNA)*

visiting his family home at Herrlingen in Bavaria, not getting back to his HQ at la Roche-Guyon château, 40 km north-west of Paris, until 1700 hours.

Despite reports of paratroopers landing all over Normandy, Seventh Army identified the Allied point of main effort (*Schwerpunkt* in German) as being in the Ste-Mère-Église region, and the American intention as cutting off the Cotentin at its narrowest point. At 0340 hours coastal batteries near le Havre reported the silhouettes of numerous ships visible by moonlight as the Allied invasion force crossed the English Channel. But at this time the Germans could not assume that the airborne landings would be followed by a seaborne invasion in the same area. However, Seventh Army planned a counter-attack to surround and destroy the Americans who had landed near Ste-Mère-Église, estimated as one division in strength. At 0235 hours, 91st Airlanding Division was ordered by LXXXIV Corps to attack from the west towards the Merderet with 1057th Grenadiers (its sole remaining infantry regiment), joined by part of 100th Panzer T/R Battalion with its French tanks. The detached I/1058th and II/1058th Grenadiers were ordered to attack southward from Montebourg to Ste-Mère-Église, but confusion and delay meant that these battalions did not move until well after dawn. The 7th Assault Battalion under *Major* Hugo Messerschmidt began to arrive from the north at noon to reinforce 1058th Grenadiers. Even without its artillery, this was a powerful battalion of 1,106 soldiers which received a commendation from Seventh Army for its part in the battle. But moving through the night it had found itself in so many encounters with mis-dropped American paratroopers that it had briefly withdrawn westward off the main road, fearing that it might be encircled.

The River Merderet, in the foreground, at Chef-du-Pont bridge, looking north-westward across the water meadow towards the Hill 30 area. In 1944 all this meadowland was under water. *(Author)*

At 0600 hours LXXXIV Corps ordered 6th Paratroop Regiment to clear the Carentan area of Allied paratroops, then to attack northwards from Carentan towards Ste-Mère-Église. Already III/6th Paratroop Regiment was heavily involved pursuing American paratroopers south-east of Carentan and, without transport and in the face of the American airborne landings and airpower, it took all day to bring the regiment together. Believing that a major airborne landing was taking place south of Carentan, 352nd Infantry Division sent Battlegroup *Meyer* the LXXXIV Corps reserve, consisting of the two-battalion 915th Grenadier Regiment plus 352nd Fusilier Battalion (the divisional reconnaissance battalion), moving off westwards towards Carentan at 0420 hours. The result was that all LXXXIV Corps reserves in the Cotentin were committed to defending against the airborne assault, leaving none to use against the beach landings when they came.

CHAPTER 4

THE UTAH BEACH LANDINGS

Sailing through the night, the first landing ships of Task Force U reached their stations in the Transport Area off Utah Beach at 0200 hours on 6 June, 17,600 metres offshore to be out of range of German coastal artillery. This coincided with the arrival of the C-47s carrying 82nd Airborne over their drop zones, and the men of Task Force U could see German tracer shells firing into the sky at the aircraft. The main assault force was carried in three US Navy Attack Transport Ships, each of which carried about 1,400 troops and 26 Landing Craft Vehicle Personnel (LCVPs), together with one Landing Ship Infantry (Large) or LSI(L), the British equivalent. Rear Admiral Moon's command ship APA-33 USS *Bayfield*, which anchored at 0229 hours with Maj Gen Collins also on board, and APA-5 USS *Barnett* carried the troops for Uncle Red Beach. APA-13 USS *Joseph T. Dickman* (converted in 1941 from the ocean liner SS *President Roosevelt*) and LSI(L) SS *Empire Gauntlet* carried the troops for Tare Green Beach. These ships were largely crewed by the US Coast Guard (only

Chaplain Major Edward J. Walters conducts a service for men of Force U on an embarkation pier at Plymouth before D-Day. *(USNA)*

Allied landing craft ready for D-Day, including LCTs (Landing Craft Tank) and LCH (Landing Craft Headquarters). Photographed at Southampton on 1 June. (*Imperial War Museum EA 23731*)

partly in the case of the *Barnett*). The larger warships including the battleships took station 11,000 metres offshore, and the destroyers about 5,000 metres offshore.

At 0309 hours the E-boats at Cherbourg were ordered to put to sea in response to the invasion alert, leaving port at 0445 hours with orders for 9th Flotilla to patrol to the west and 5th Flotilla to the east, but a combination of bad weather and high seas forced them back to harbour by dawn. Meanwhile at 0335 hours the Allied bombing intensified as 1,327 RAF Bomber Command aircraft attacked targets across Lower Normandy. At Crisbecq, the casemated battery was hit by 600 tons of bombs, destroying its anti-aircraft guns. Mis-dropped groups of paratroopers, chiefly from 502nd PIR, also attacked the battery, which took twenty of the Americans prisoner that night.

The German Air Force made no appearance over Utah until the evening when a few aircraft made strafing runs over the beach. Allied fighter cover over the naval flotilla for D-Day, including Task Force U, was provided by four squadrons of distinctive twin-boomed USAAF P-38 Lightnings, which could not be mistaken for German aircraft. From dawn onwards on D-Day six squadrons of RAF Spitfires provided low cover and three squadrons of USAAF P-47 Thunderbolts provided high cover over the landing beaches. Additional fighter cover was divided between the beaches and inland areas: one Thunderbolt squadron covered the Western Task Force area, and a Spitfire squadron was assigned to each of the Utah and Omaha beaches.

The first D-Day landing from the sea at Utah Beach took place in darkness at 0430 hours, when 132 officers and men of A Troop, 4th Cavalry Squadron, and B Troop, 24th Cavalry Squadron, under Lt Col Edward C. Dunn landed unopposed on the Îles St-Marcouf in rubber rafts and assault craft from LSI(L) SS *Empire Gauntlet*. The cavalrymen lost five officers and men to land mines in securing the islands by 0530 hours, and a total of nineteen killed or wounded, being relieved next day.

A German shell exploding close to a Landing Ship Tank (LST) off Utah Beach in the early stages of the D-Day landing. *(USNA)*

Meanwhile at 0405 hours the landing craft for the main assault began to be lowered from the landing ships, joining the LCTs that had crossed the Channel. Thirty minutes later the first waves set off for their long and rough journey in the choppy grey seas to the line of departure at the edge of Area Vermont, where the craft kept station before being signalled to go forward to land. Landing craft at Utah were crewed by the US Navy, US

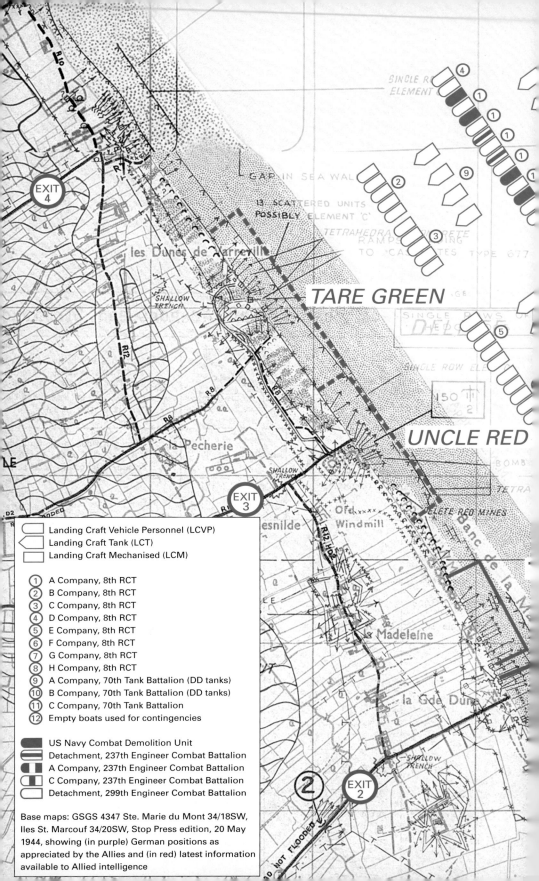

EXIT
4

les Dunes de Varreville

SHALLOW
TRENCH

R12

R8

R8

la Pecherie

SHALLOW
TRENCH

EXIT
3

CAPTAIN SEA WALL

13 SCATTERED UNITS
POSSIBLY ELEMENT 'C'

TETRAHEDRA CONCRETE
RAMPS LEADING
TO CASEMATES TYPE 677

TARE GREEN

SINGLE ROWS OF
DELETE

SINGLE ROW ELE

N50

UNCLE RED

BOMB

TETRA

DELETE RED MINES

Banc de la M

esnilde

Old
Windmill

R12 H02

le Madeleine

la Gde Dun

SHALLOW
TRENCH

2

EXIT
2

NOT FLOODED

Landing Craft Vehicle Personnel (LCVP)
Landing Craft Tank (LCT)
Landing Craft Mechanised (LCM)

(1) A Company, 8th RCT
(2) B Company, 8th RCT
(3) C Company, 8th RCT
(4) D Company, 8th RCT
(5) E Company, 8th RCT
(6) F Company, 8th RCT
(7) G Company, 8th RCT
(8) H Company, 8th RCT
(9) A Company, 70th Tank Battalion (DD tanks)
(10) B Company, 70th Tank Battalion (DD tanks)
(11) C Company, 70th Tank Battalion
(12) Empty boats used for contingencies

US Navy Combat Demolition Unit
Detachment, 237th Engineer Combat Battalion
A Company, 237th Engineer Combat Battalion
C Company, 237th Engineer Combat Battalion
Detachment, 299th Engineer Combat Battalion

Base maps: GSGS 4347 Ste. Marie du Mont 34/18SW,
Iles St. Marcouf 34/20SW, Stop Press edition, 20 May
1944, showing (in purple) German positions as
appreciated by the Allies and (in red) latest information
available to Allied intelligence

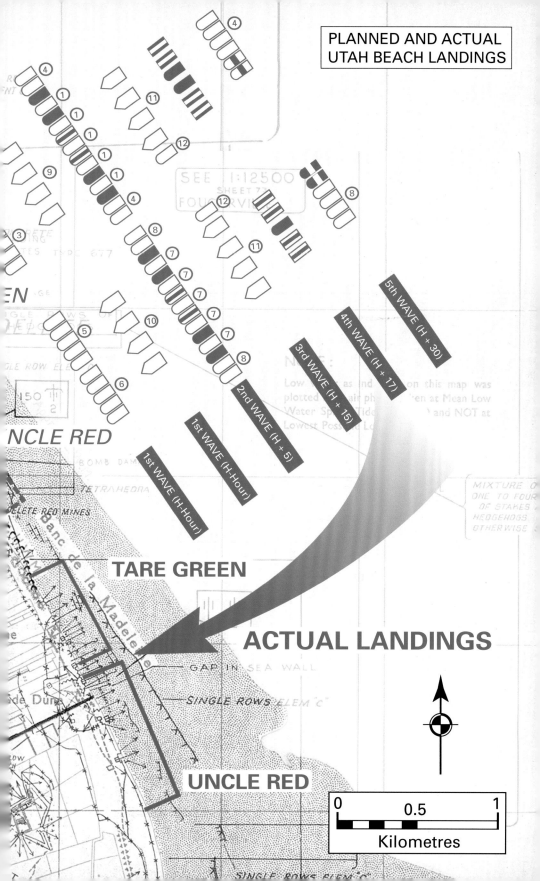

PLANNED AND ACTUAL
UTAH BEACH LANDINGS

Order of Battle, Utah Beach Landing Forces

VII Corps *Maj Gen J. Lawton Collins*

4th Infantry Division *Maj Gen Raymond O. Barton*
Assistant Commander: *Brig Gen Theodore Roosevelt Jr.*

8th Infantry Regt, 12th Infantry Regt, 22nd Infantry Regt
20th Field Artillery Battalion, 29th Field Artillery Battalion,
42nd Field Artillery Battalion, 44th Field Artillery Battalion
4th Engineer Combat Battalion

Attached Units:
65th Armored Field Artillery Btn, 87th Armored Field Artillery Btn,
801st Tank Destroyer Battalion, 87th Chemical Weapons Battalion,
1106th Engineer Combat Group, 980th Field Artillery Battalion
(1 battery), 13th Field Artillery Observation Battalion,
Company C 320th Barrage Balloon Battalion (VLA) (Colored)

359th Infantry Regiment (from 90th Infantry Division)

4th Cavalry Group
4th Cavalry Squadron, 24th Cavalry Squadron

6th Armored Group
70th Tank Battalion, 746th Tank Battalion, 749th Tank Battalion,
899th Tank Destroyer Battalion

11th Anti-Aircraft Artillery Group
116th AAA Btn, 535th AAA Automatic Weapons Battalion,
474th AAA Automatic Weapons Self Propelled Battalion

1st Engineer Special Brigade* *Brig Gen James E. Wharton*
HQ & HQ Company, 531st Engineer Shore Regt (3 shore btns),
24th Amphibious Truck Battalion (462nd, 478th, 479th Companies),
306th QM Battalion (556th & 562nd QM Railhead Companies,
393rd QM Gas Supply Company), 191st Ordnance Battalion
(3497th Ordnance MAM Company, 625th Ordnance Ammunition
Company, 161st Ordnance Platoon), 577th QM Battalion
(363d, 3207th, 4144th QM Service Co), 261st Medical Battalion,
449th Military Police Company, 286th JASCO, 33rd Chemical
Decontamination Company, 3206th QM Service Company
** Plus attached units: the full list for all the units of this brigade is on its
memorial at Utah Beach*

US Navy 2nd Naval Beach Battalion

Naval Combat Demolition Units

Key: AAA Anti-Aircraft Artillery, JASCO Joint Assault Signal Company,
MAM Medium Automotive Maintenance, QM Quartermaster,
VLA Very Low Altitude.

Coast Guard and some Royal Navy crews. The assault waves consisted chiefly of LCVPs each carrying up to 36 men or one vehicle (sometimes called 'Higgins Boats' from their American designer, Andrew Higgins), together with the LCTs carrying armoured vehicles, and Landing Craft Mechanised (LCMs).

These were supported by M7 Priest 105-mm self-propelled guns and M4 Sherman tanks landing from LCTs, including in the first wave amphibious or DD Shermans (for 'Duplex Drive') fitted with propellers and waterproofing, meant to be launched from their LCTs about 5,000 metres offshore and to swim onto the beach. Further support came from LCG(L)s with 4.7-inch naval guns and LCF (Flak) with anti-aircraft guns, and the spectacular LCT(R) landing craft fitted with racks for 1,096 5-inch rockets that were fired in salvoes in a matter of seconds.

A typical element of a *Wiederstandnest* (resistance nest) on Utah Beach. This example is at Quinéville. *(Author)*

The LCTs carrying the DD Shermans arrived in the Transport Area at 0445 hours and continued onwards towards the beach, led in by LCS (Small). US Navy PT boats (fast torpedo boats) and Patrol Craft (PC) marked the edge of the landing area to prevent any craft straying too far north. Signals to each wave of landing craft were given by lights from the Landing Craft Control (LCC), equipped with radar and captained by members of the US Navy's Scouts and Raiders, specialists in amphibious operations. Tare Green was assigned to PC 1176, LCC-60 and LCC-70, Uncle Red to PC 1261, LCC-80 and LCC-90. The PCs for each beach were to mark the line of departure while one LCC guided the landing craft in and the other kept station in the Transport Area.

The reinforced 4th Infantry Division was a Regular Army division known as the 'Ivy Division' from its four-leaf divisional sign. On both the American beaches the first three-battalion regiment that led the assault was reorganised as a Regimental Combat Team (RCT), with each battalion divided into Infantry Assault Teams (also known as Assault Boat Teams) including heavy weapons such as flame throwers and demolition charges to help clear the beach defences. The first wave of landing troops at Utah was provided by 8th RCT of 4th Infantry Division under Colonel James Van Fleet. B and C Companies of 1/8th RCT in ten LCVPs under Lt Col Conrad Simmons landed in the first wave at Tare Green, supported by A Company, 70th Tank Battalion, including DD Shermans. E and F Companies, 2/8th RCT, also in ten LCVPs under Lt Col Carlton MacNeely, landed at Uncle Red supported by B Company, 70th Tank Battalion, including DD Shermans, followed by the specialist Beach Obstacle Demolition Parties (BODP) of the Provisional Battalion, 1106th Engineer Combat Group (237th Engineer Combat Battalion reinforced by B Company, 299th Engineer Combat Battalion, and other specialist troops), under Major Herschel Linn. The BODP included eleven US Navy Combat Demolition Units (NCDU) each of sixteen men under Lieutenant Commander Herbert Peterson, made up of Gap Assault Teams and Support Teams with explosives to clear the way through German obstacles. Behind the first line of landing troops, the immediate support line was the remainder of 1/8th RCT (A and D Companies) for Tare Green and 2/8th RCT (G and H Companies) for Uncle Red, with C Company, 70th Tank Battalion, including 'tankdozers' or armoured bulldozers (the battalion's light M5 Stuart tanks landed with a later wave).

Shortly after 0505 hours the German coastal batteries opened fire on the destroyers USS *Fitch* and USS *Corry*, starting an exchange of shells, and the formal order for Bombardment Force A to open fire was given at 0536 hours. The pre-planned naval bombardment began at 0550, with some warships firing at batteries far away along the coast on either side of the landing area. The 2/1261st Coastal Artillery battery at Azeville was hit by the 14-inch guns of the battleship USS *Nevada*, but remained firing. The German Navy battery at Crisbecq was fired upon by the cruiser USS *Quincy* and returned fire at the *Nevada*, which also replied. Those German batteries protected only by earth and timber suffered heavily in the bombardment; afterwards the battery site at Fontenay-sur-Mer was described as resembling a ploughed field. Fire from the British cruiser HMS *Enterprise*, the

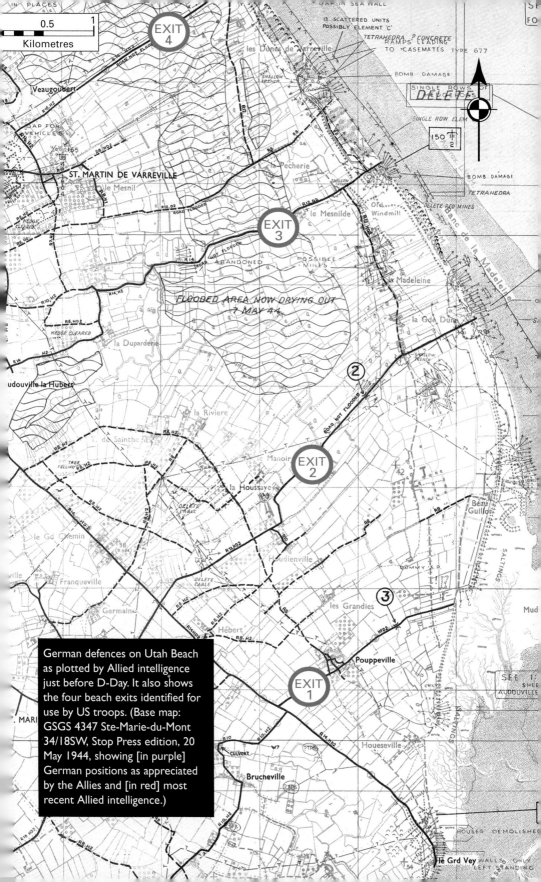

German defences on Utah Beach as plotted by Allied intelligence just before D-Day. It also shows the four beach exits identified for use by US troops. (Base map: GSGS 4347 Ste-Marie-du-Mont 34/18SW, Stop Press edition, 20 May 1944, showing [in purple] German positions as appreciated by the Allies and [in red] most recent Allied intelligence.)

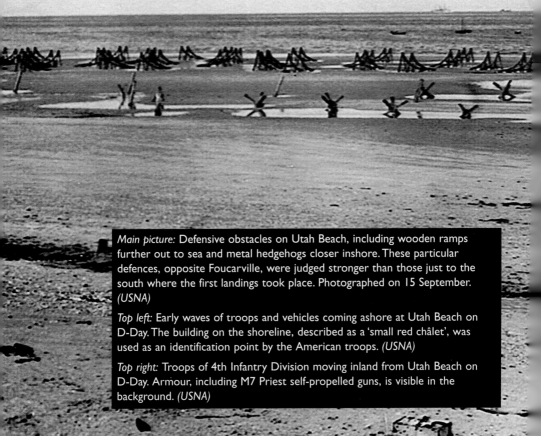

Main picture: Defensive obstacles on Utah Beach, including wooden ramps further out to sea and metal hedgehogs closer inshore. These particular defences, opposite Foucarville, were judged stronger than those just to the south where the first landings took place. Photographed on 15 September. *(USNA)*

Top left: Early waves of troops and vehicles coming ashore at Utah Beach on D-Day. The building on the shoreline, described as a 'small red châlet', was used as an identification point by the American troops. *(USNA)*

Top right: Troops of 4th Infantry Division moving inland from Utah Beach on D-Day. Armour, including M7 Priest self-propelled guns, is visible in the background. *(USNA)*

Dutch sloop HNMS *Soemba*, and the destroyers inshore was directed at the resistance nests and strongpoints along Utah Beach, exploding minefields and wrecking bunkers.

The heavily overcast dawn came at 0556 hours, with continuing rain and scattered low clouds (between 2,000 and 3,000 feet). From then until 0610 hours, 276 B-26 Marauder bombers of US Ninth Air Force dropped 4,400 250-lb bombs onto the German positions at Utah Beach; a further 67 aircraft failed to bomb because of the overcast. Targets were hard to identify, and about a third of the bombs missed the German resistance nests. US Navy pilots of Squadron VCS-7 (specially formed for the invasion) flying Spitfires acted as observers over the beaches together with their RAF counterparts. Allied Intelligence later found that about half of all German batteries captured in the Utah battles had guns still capable of firing; but the devastating impact of the Allied air and naval bombardment had greatly reduced their ability to fight back.

As the first wave of 20 LCVPs approached the shore with a second wave of 32 LCVPs immediately behind them, some of the Shermans of 70th Tank Battalion in LCT(A) – for armoured – opened fire over the bows of their craft onto the beach. The LCG(L)s on the flanks of each assault wave targeted the resistance nests with their 4.7-inch guns as they came within range. The M7 Priest 105-mm self-propelled guns of 65th Armored Field Artillery Battalion were also intended to fire over the bows of the LCTs until the range got too close, but reportedly failed to do so due to confusion with the signals given to them. At about 3,000 metres, 17 LCT(R)s fired off their 'drenching' salvoes of rockets, each smothering an area 750 by 160 metres in just 90 seconds, although many of the rockets fell short of the beach. At 400 metres from the shore smoke projectors were fired as a signal for the offshore naval bombardment to cease.

The effect on the German defences of the combined attack from aircraft, naval gunnery and the final assault bombardment was devastating. At WN-5/WN-104 defending Exit 2, the air attacks damaged the 88-mm gun, and destroyed one 75-mm gun and the two 50-mm anti-tank guns, together with machine-gun nests, an ammunition bunker and the control mechanisms for all the Goliath miniature tanks. As the LCVPs approached, the naval bombardment destroyed the remaining 75-mm gun and the controls for the flame throwers, as well as blasting mines, barbed wire, trenches and bunkers, leaving *Leutnant* Jahnke's men dead, injured, scared and shaken – in some cases to the point of breakdown. Other than the damaged 88-mm gun and an 80-mm mortar emplacement, all their heavy weapons were gone.

Smoke, spray, and overcast, with a strong wind and tide on a choppy sea, were not ideal landing conditions with few landmarks to guide the craft, and there was inevitable confusion as the first wave approached. PC 1261, the patrol craft assigned to 2/8th RCT heading for Uncle Red beach, was sunk by either a shell or a mine at 0542 hours, the control craft LCC-80 had failed to make the Channel crossing due to mechanical problems,

A pillbox, part of the WN-5/WN-104 defences opposite the first American landings on Utah Beach, with a dead German defender outside. *(USNA)*

and LCC-90 remained in the Transport Area. This left PC 1176 under Lieutenant John B. Ricker and LCC-60 under Lieutenants Sims S. Gauthier and Howard Vander Beek directing 1/8th RCT to Tare Green beach to direct 2/8th RCT to Uncle Red as well. Given the bad sea state, the low-freeboard DD Shermans were not launched until they were between 3,000 and 1,500 metres from shore and their LCTs got ahead of the leading LCVPs, some of which needed to steer round the swimming tanks after their launch, further disrupting the timings and direction of movement.

The Allies originally planned for the Utah Beach landings to take place north of la Grande Dune at les Dunes de Varreville, but most accounts agree that the strong current and winds pushed the landing craft southwards, and that the first waves of 1/8th RCT and 2/8th RCT touched down a few minutes after their planned landing time of 0630 hours, on either side of Exit 2 at la Grande Dune close to the hamlet of la Madeleine and in front of *Leutnant* Jahnke's battered WN-5/WN-104, some 2,000 metres south of their planned landing position. Seven landing craft were lost. Planned to land ahead of the first infantry, the DD Shermans mostly landed a few minutes behind them, but all made it to the beach except four on board an LCT which hit a mine before they could launch. The LCTs carrying C Company's

Medics at work with the wounded on Utah Beach on 6 June. (USNA)

tanks, including six tankdozers, reached the shore at about the same time, also for the loss of four tanks. Wading through the waist-high water, the troops were on the beach with the four planned exit causeway roads to their front as intended.

The troops manning WN-5/WN-104 fought back against this overwhelming onslaught of firepower and determined Americans as best they could. The damaged 88-mm gun hit one Sherman before its barrel blew out, and the machine gunner in the Renault-turreted Tobruk pit kept firing as long as possible. The expected fire support from the 122-mm battery of 1/1261st Coastal Artillery at St-Martin-de-Varreville did not come, since the battery had long been bombed and abandoned, and its location had already been secured by American paratroopers. But, as the first troops of 4th Infantry Division landed and began fighting for the beaches, it was still not clear how well the night's airborne landings had succeeded.

CHAPTER 5

THE D-DAY FIGHTING

Inland after dawn, as the light improved over the Cotentin and many landmarks (particularly church towers and steeples) became more obvious, the small groups of American paratroopers which had assembled began to reach their objectives. Those airborne battalions that gathered into units for the morning of D-Day fought between fifteen and twenty separate battles altogether, each starting with 100 men or fewer (usually from more than one regiment or even division) and finishing the day with perhaps 400 effectives. All these actions contributed to the American victory on D-Day, and many have since been analysed and reconstructed in detail.

At 0354 hours, still in darkness and moonlight, the first of 52 USAAF CG-4A Waco gliders, each towed by a C-47, arrived from England after a flight of 71 minutes, approaching directly from the east rather than from the west as the C-47s carrying the paratroopers had done earlier. They were aiming for the landing zone designated LZ E (an extension to the west of DZ C) carrying 158 men with sixteen 57-mm anti-tank guns, a bulldozer, and medical and signal equipment for 101st Airborne. Simultaneously, 52 Waco gliders flew in aiming for LZ O, with 22 jeeps and sixteen 57-mm anti-tank guns for 82nd Airborne. The airborne divisions had code-named each of their glider landings after towns and cities in the United States, and this was the critical 'Chicago Mission', to provide the paratroopers on the

HISTORY

ground with heavy weapons and reinforcements. Despite accurate marking, coming down into small fields covered with glider poles carried a very high risk. Only six gliders landed on LZ E, and there were at least 17 injuries and 5 deaths, among them the assistant divisional commander of 101st Airborne, Brig Gen Donald F. Pratt, who was one of those killed. The gliders intended for the 82nd Airborne did rather better. Twenty-three gliders landed on DZ/LZ O, and two crashed into Ste-Mère-Église; 26 soldiers became casualties, and 11 jeeps and 8 guns were recovered. The 57-mm anti-tank guns played an important role in the American defence, particularly at la Fière and Chef-du-Pont and at the hamlet of Neuville-au-Plain north of Ste-Mère-Église, providing extra support against German armoured vehicles for the paratroopers.

One of the small groups of American paratroopers who gathered together to fight on D-Day, taking a rest in one of the little villages near Utah beach on D-Day. *(USNA)*

Closest to the beaches, 101st Airborne had achieved its main objectives despite its lack of numbers. Forty-three men of 3/506th PIR under Captain Charles Shettle secured the bridges over the River Taute near Brévands at 0430 hours, although the force was too weak to hold the eastern bank also. Colonel Howard 'Skeets' Johnson, commanding 501st PIR, with 150 men captured

A Horsa glider on the ground in a field close to Utah Beach. The closeness of the trees and hedgerows to the glider shows some of the dangers of landing. Photograph taken on 8 July. *(USNA)*

la Barquette lock, linking up by 0900 hours with other groups from 501st PIR and pressing westwards to engage 3/1058th Grenadier Regiment near St-Côme-du-Mont. Various small groups and individuals including Maj Gen Taylor moved towards Exit 1 at Pouppeville, reached by about 200 men chiefly from 1/506th PIR and 3/501st PIR. Taylor's divisional headquarters staff and company, largely composed of clerks and specialists not usually meant to fight, received a Unit Citation for D-Day.

The inundations between Exits 3 and 2, together with artillery fire and the presence of 795th Georgian Battalion, held up movement from the north towards Exit 2 (Seventh Army headquarters later commended the unexpectedly high fighting qualities of its *Ost* battalions), but troops from 2/506th PIR under Lt Col Robert Strayer reached the exit road at 1330 hours.

Lt Col Robert Cole, commanding 3/502nd PIR, collected 75 men in a circuitous march through the dark going as far west as Ste-Mère-Église at one point, but by 0730 hours his force was in position and dug in covering Exit 3 and Exit 4. Lt Col Steve Chappuis and men of 2/502nd PIR reached their objective, the 1/1261st Coastal Artillery position at St-Martin-de-Varreville, to find it wrecked and abandoned. Allied bombing had destroyed the battery fire control, and the guns had been relocated. Lt Col 'Pat' Cassidy of 1/502nd PIR collected a similarly sized force and moved first to the farmhouses at WXYZ, where building W was commandeered as a temporary headquarters. Cassidy's position close to Mézières became a point of contact for men of the division moving through in search of their units. The farmhouse buildings at XYZ were cleared in a series of firefights lasting until 1530 hours. Meanwhile, 1/502nd PIR had established a position to the north at Foucarville, coming under fire throughout the day from 1058th Grenadiers from the north.

On Utah Beach itself the events of the morning were also going well for the Americans, although landing on the wrong beach threw out some of the planned timings as each successive wave of landing craft assembled and headed inshore. Estimates of exactly where troops came ashore later varied, and there was at least one account (not officially confirmed) that some men landed on the original planned beach and fought there. Landing with the first wave of 2/8th Infantry was 4th Infantry Division's assistant commander, Brig Gen 'Teddy' Roosevelt, 57 years old and son of former President Theodore Roosevelt (after whom the *Joseph T. Dickman* had been named in its original existence). His son Captain Quentin Roosevelt also landed on Omaha Beach during D-Day.

Brig Gen Teddy Roosevelt. This picture shows him on 12 July, the day that he suffered his fatal heart attack. *(USNA)*

At 0720 hours the first troops of 87th Chemical Weapons Battalion came ashore with their 4.2-inch mortars ('chemical' because their original planned use had been for smoke) to provide some firepower. The second wave was due to arrive at 0745 hours, still heading for the original beach, consisting of the rest of 299th Engineer Combat Battalion (299th ECB), 3/22nd

A 4.2-inch mortar in action on Utah Beach on D-Day. *(USNA)*

Infantry and 1/22nd Infantry at Tare Green, and the rest of 237th ECB, 3/8th Infantry and 2/22nd Infantry at Uncle Red. On the beach, Brig Gen Roosevelt agreed with Colonel Van Fleet and his two battalion commanders that it was better to continue the landings where they were – redesignated the new Uncle Red and Tare Green – than to land the second wave as planned and try to link up. For his bravery on Utah Beach on D-Day, Teddy Roosevelt was awarded the Medal of Honor; he died of a heart attack in Normandy on 12 July before receiving it.

The sudden change in direction to the new beach as the landing craft made their last run-in had the advantage that much of the German artillery continued to fire on the original beach position, and that the beach obstacles were fewer than further north. Two waves of specialists from the NCDU followed over the next half hour with plans to clear four lanes each 50 metres wide through the obstacles on the beach and inland, together with Major Linn's engineers (without the major himself, whose craft was sunk on the approach; he landed at Utah next day). But the beach defences were so weak that it was judged easier to clear them completely rather than clearing lanes. A critical role was played by 1st Engineer Special Brigade (1st ESB) under Brig Gen James E. Wharton, with specialised units including military police, ordnance, signals, medical, and combat engineering. The first units of 1st ESB to land were 1st and 2nd Battalions of 531st Engineer Shore Regiment. By 0800 hours, despite three tankdozers being lost, over 700 metres of beach had been cleared. The strongpoint at la Madeleine and others to the north were soon captured. The engineers blew gaps through the sea wall and began clearing the mines from the causeway roads. At 0900 hours the infantry and tanks began to move off the beach, 1/8th Infantry down Exit 3 and 2/8th Infantry with most of 70th Tank Battalion down Exit 1. By 0930 hours, three hours after the first landings, the beach was clear of obstacles.

Cleared obstacles piled together on Utah Beach. Photographed on 8 June. *(USNA)*

Altogether on D-Day, 4th Infantry Division came ashore with twelve infantry battalions in six two-battalion waves, together with armour and supporting troops, the main waves subdivided into 26 lines of landing craft. Three waves each of two battalions were planned to land at 1000 hours and then 30 and 40 minutes later, including 4th Infantry Division's third regiment, 12th Infantry. Landing side by side with 3/12th Infantry was 1st Battalion of 401st Glider Infantry Regiment (1/401st GIR; which was attached to 327th GIR as its third battalion but preferred to keep its original title), followed in the final wave by 1/359th Infantry and 3/359th Infantry from 90th Infantry Division, attached to 4th Infantry Division for D-Day.

The beach area at WN-5/WN/104 was still under direct German fire, and remained under artillery fire for several days. At about 0730 hours the destroyer USS *Corry* had gone down, probably from fire from the Crisbecq battery (although the *Corry* may have hit a mine, both the Crisbecq battery and 4/1261st Coastal Artillery at Quinéville reported sinking a 'small cruiser'); 30 minutes later return fire put one of the Crisbecq battery's 210-mm guns out of action, and at 0900 hours the shelling destroyed a second 210-mm gun. The 105-mm Priests of 65th Armored Field Artillery Battalion were all ashore by 0930 hours, remaining on the beach and providing fire support until about 1730 hours when they began to move inland. Shore Fire Control Parties also landed with the first wave to direct naval gunfire, work which would become critical in the fighting later in the day.

A Shore Fire Control Party directing naval gunfire in the Utah Beach landing area. Photographed on 10 June. *(USNA)*

HISTORY

At 1025 hours Colonel Van Fleet radioed to Maj Gen 'Tubby' Barton commanding 4th Infantry Division, 'Everything is going OK.' By 1200 hours all the battalions of 8th Infantry and 22nd Infantry with their supports were ashore, and the survivors of WN-5/WN-104 were being rounded up, including the wounded *Leutnant* Jahnke. Colonel Eugene M. Caffey, deputy commander of 1st Engineer Special Brigade, raised the first Stars and Stripes flag over Utah Beach. Maj Gen Barton landed with his staff at 1400 hours to set up his headquarters.

Prisoners from WN-5/WN-104 under escort by men of 8th Infantry Regiment. *(USNA)*

The divisional plan was for each regiment to advance with two battalions leading and one in reserve. The D-Day objectives were that 3/8th Infantry and 2/8th Infantry would first move westward to the main Cherbourg road, between St-Côme-du-Mont and the next main crossroads northwards at les Forges, ready to push further west to reach 82nd Airborne. Next, 22nd Infantry would advance northwards to seize the high ground at Quinéville as far inland as the coastal ridge road; and then 12th Infantry would move north-westwards to reach the main Cherbourg road at Edmondeville (half-way between Ste-Mère-Église and

Montebourg) and the high ground beyond as far as the Merderet; 359th Infantry was kept as divisional reserve at Foucarville.

Meanwhile, 82nd Airborne remained isolated from events at Utah Beach and out of radio communications with VII Corps. Maj Gen Ridgway could transmit messages, but he was not receiving any. Many of his men were cut off west of the Merderet for several days, though some groups were large enough to help blunt the counter-attacks from 1057th Grenadiers. The largest was a force under Lt Col 'Terrible Tom' Shanley of 2/508th PIR, which increased to two companies in the course of D-Day. The men of this group established themselves in an all-round defence at 'Hill 30' a protrusion of hard ground covered by apple trees and hedgerows rising from the swamp on the west bank of the Merderet between la Fière and Chef-du-Pont.

During the morning different groups from all three infantry regiments of 82nd Airborne, including many that had crossed the swamp from the west, congregated on the east bank of the causeway near la Fière farmhouse under Brig Gen Gavin, starting with troops from 1/505th PIR and finally numbering about 300 men. As in other fights on D-Day and later, the blind nature of the hedgerow country often prevented isolated groups of American soldiers from realising that they were fighting towards the same objective. After a protracted firefight in the hedgerows at la Fière, by noon the farmhouse was captured, and found to have been defended by only 28 men of 1057th Grenadiers.

Meanwhile, the church and tiny hamlet of Cauquigny on the west side of the causeway had been captured during the morning by men of 2/507th PIR under Lt Col Charles Timmes. But these decided to press on towards their objective at the next village of Amfreville, leaving only a token force behind. At 1345 hours more men of 2/507th PIR made their way westward across the causeway from la Fière to Cauquigny, but these also continued on towards Amfreville. Before a proper defence could be organised at Cauquigny, at about 1400 hours troops of 1057th Grenadiers with a few French-made Renault R35 tanks of 100th Panzer T/R Battalion attacked and captured the Cauquigny end of the causeway, leaving the Americans near Amfreville cut off, including 120 men under Lt Col Timmes in a nearby orchard. At 1730 hours the Germans made the first of a series of attacks with tanks and infantry down the causeway towards la Fière. These lasted until 2000 hours, and were only just held by an improvised force, mainly from 1/505th PIR, with a few mines and anti-tank weapons. This loss of the Merderet causeway on D-Day would mean hard fighting for the Americans over the next few days.

Meanwhile to the south-west another intense fight had developed at the bridge at Chef-du-Pont. At 0900 hours Brig Gen Gavin ordered about 150 men from la Fière in two groups southward in an attempt to rush the Chef-du-Pont bridge, a humped-back stone structure crossing over the flooded Merderet south-west of the village. This led to a protracted firefight as more men arrived and were deployed on both sides. The Americans finally secured the bridge for the loss of 11 dead and 23 wounded, finding 40 German dead. At 1730 hours, learning of the German attacks across the la Fière causeway, Gavin ordered most of the troops from 507th PIR at Chef-du-Pont back northwards to la Fière, leaving 34 men under Captain Roy E. Creek defending the east side of the bridge. A few minutes later, 1057th Grenadiers launched their major attack of the day at Chef-du-Pont, supported by artillery, but could not force their way across the bridge against Creek's paratroopers. American reinforcements arrived shortly afterwards, and at dusk the paratroopers were still holding Chef-du-Pont bridge.

With so few troops available after the scattered landings, securing Ste-Mère-Église became of much greater importance for 82nd Airborne. Once on the ground, 3/505th PIR under Lt Col Edward 'Cannonball' Krause, with 108 men led by a French guide, moved off towards Ste-Mère-Église. In an attack using only bayonets, knives and grenades in the dark (so that any firing could be treated as hostile) they captured the town by 0430 hours, and cut the main German communications cable to Cherbourg. The German garrison largely retreated southwards. At 0500 hours, 2/505th PIR under Lt Col 'Ben' Vandervoort (whose injured leg prevented his walking properly) moved off north towards the village of Neuville-au-Plain to block the main road to Montebourg. After some changes of direction and orders, Vandervoort's force was ordered south to Ste-Mère-Église by Colonel William Ekman commanding 505th PIR, leaving only a platoon of 42 men just north of Neuville. German counter-attacks from the north towards Ste-Mère-Église began at 1030 hours as the leading company of 1058th Grenadiers reached Neuville, starting a firefight in the hedgerows that lasted until late afternoon when 16 American survivors pulled back.

Men of 82nd Airborne Division entering Ste-Mère-Église on the morning of D-Day. *(USNA)*

The first German local counter-attack from the south began shortly after 0930 hours, described by the Americans as the most serious threat to Ste-Mère-Église that day, with a strength of at least two companies supported by tanks or assault guns and artillery. The only German troops in the locality so early on D-Day were 795th Georgian Battalion to the south-east, III/1058th Grenadiers to the south, and the remnants of the town garrison; some armour from 100th Panzer T/R Battalion may well have reached them. In response, Lt Col Krause moved 3/505th PIR to defend the southern approaches to Ste-Mère-Église, and Vandervoort's 2/505th PIR arrived to defend the northern approaches. By the afternoon the German attack had spent itself, leaving the Americans firmly in control of the town. Thereafter, 2/505th PIR and 3/505th PIR reported nothing but German patrols from the south for the rest of the day.

Since 0900 hours a fight had also been in progress at Pouppeville between about 70 Germans of III/1058th Grenadiers and troops from 1/501st PIR under Lt Col Julian Ewell. The first tank of 70th Tank Battalion from Utah Beach appeared along the Exit 1 road at about 1100 hours and, as 2/8th Infantry moved up Exit 1, the Germans surrendered at noon, realising they were surrounded. This was the first link-up between the airborne forces and troops from Utah Beach on D-Day. At Exit 3, at 0930 hours, Germans trying to retreat inland were ambushed by Lt Col Cole's 3/502nd PIR group, who killed over 50 without loss. At the same time 49th ECB and 238th ECB landed at Utah to repair and strengthen the exit roads and build temporary bridges across obstacles, and by 1300 hours 1/8th Infantry following up along Exit 3 had also linked up with the paratroopers.

US combat engineers improving a dirt road inland from Utah Beach using armoured bulldozers on 8 June. (USNA)

Troops of 506th PIR spent several hours over-running German positions west of Ste-Marie-du-Mont, including the batteries of II/191st Artillery (which had not been properly identified by Allied Intelligence before D-Day), before advancing on the village and linking up with 3/8th Infantry. Pushing northwards along the coast, 3/22nd Infantry engaged the remaining resistance nests, although Exit 4 remained under fire from some German positions and could not be used. This led to 1/22nd Infantry and 2/22nd Infantry wading through the swamps north of Exit 3 to reach the ridge road, followed by the three battalions of 12th Infantry to the south of the exit road.

An M4 Sherman tank *Hurricane* of 746th Tank Battalion disembarking on Utah Beach on D-Day. *(USNA)*

The rest of 4th Infantry Division, including its artillery, continued to come ashore, followed by more elements of VII Corps including 746th Tank Battalion and the first two companies of 899th Tank Destroyer Battalion with its M10 Wolverines (often confused with Shermans at first glance), and more engineers of 1106th Engineer Combat Group. Noteworthy landings at Utah on D-Day included Battery C, 320th Barrage Balloon Battalion (VLA) (Colored), composed of African-Americans in the still segregated US Army, with their 'very low altitude' barrage balloons, and Colonel James E. Kerr, a member of Rear Admiral Moon's staff, believed to be the only US Marine to land on D-Day. Ship-to-shore communications up to the high water mark were handled from the beach by the US Navy's 2nd Naval Beach Battalion under its Beachmaster, part of 1st

Engineer Special Brigade. Army communications were handled by another unit of 1st ESB, 286th Joint Assault Signal Company. Units of 1st ESB began to establish ammunition, fuel, and supply dumps, starting the process of transforming the beach battlefield into a maintenance area. German artillery, and an attack by a few German aircraft late in the day, cost 1st ESB 21 killed and 91 wounded on D-Day.

A heavy weapons unit of 90th Infantry Division advancing along a dirt road in hedgerow country inland from Utah Beach on D-Day. *(USNA)*

In addition to the difficulties at Exit 4, German artillery fire still prevented VII Corps from using Exit 3 for vehicles as planned, and there were some delays on Exit 2 due to a destroyed culvert, leading to congestion and traffic jams on the beach. But the landing continued to go extremely well for the Americans. Command posts for 4th Infantry Division and an advanced detachment of VII Corps were established near Exit 3. As the afternoon and early evening progressed, 1/8th Infantry advanced due west from Exit 3 to a position directly opposing 795th Georgian Battalion at Turqueville. At 1650 hours contact was made between patrols from 1/8th Infantry and 505th PIR from

Ste-Mère-Église. By 2100 hours, 1/22nd Infantry had reached St-Germain-de-Varreville as the eastern anchor of an American line facing northwards against 1058th Grenadiers and 7th Assault Battalion, with 2/22nd Infantry to its west, then 1/12th and 2/12th Infantry, with 3/12th Infantry in reserve. Late in the evening a patrol from 82nd Airborne led by Lt Col W.F. Winton made contact with 12th Infantry, and reached Maj Gen Barton's command post at midnight. Full radio communications with 82nd Airborne Division's headquarters were established at 0929 hours next day when it received the signal, 'No info on your locations. All headquarters deeply concerned.'

Paratroopers of 101st Airborne Division with locals in the main square at Ste-Marie-du-Mont on 7 June. (USNA)

Also moving off from Exit 2 on the afternoon of D-Day, 3/8th Infantry helped clear the area around Ste-Marie-du-Mont and drove on to les Forges crossroads on the main Cherbourg road. Driving rapidly westward from Pouppeville and leaving German strongpoints to the south to be captured next day, 2/8th Infantry with most of 70th Tank Battalion also reached the main Cherbourg road to the south of les Forges by 1900 hours, supported by 29th Field Artillery Battalion, thus effectively surrounding 795th Georgian Battalion from the south and east. Patrols from 3/8th Infantry and from 82nd Airborne established contact between les Forges and Chef-du-Pont. Then 'Howell

Force' under Colonel Edison D. Raff (comprising a platoon of armoured cars from B Company of 4th Cavalry Squadron, C Company of 746th Tank Battalion and 90 men of 325th GIR riding on the Sherman tanks) which had landed at Utah Beach at 1550 hours, attempted to push on westward past les Forges to reinforce the 82nd Airborne. But this attempt was checked by 100th Panzer T/R Battalion and 1057th Grenadiers with artillery support. This left LZ W at les Forges, intended for further glider landings, in no-man's-land between the Americans and Germans.

An Airspeed Horsa glider on the ground in Normandy, showing how its detachable tail was used to ease unloading. Photograph taken 12 June. *(USNA)*

By 1800 hours on D-Day, 21,328 troops, 1,742 vehicles, and 1,695 tons of stores had been landed from the sea at Utah Beach. The troops of VII Corps were holding a beachhead of about 4 km and had penetrated more than 8 km inland, linking up with 101st Airborne Division. But there was no continuous front yet established, and 82nd Airborne Division was still largely on its own. Total casualties for 4th Infantry Division were 197 killed, wounded and missing, including 60 men lost at sea. Within the division, losses for 8th Infantry were 5 killed, 60 wounded and 13 missing, and for 22nd Infantry 7 killed and 46 wounded.

For an opposed amphibious landing these losses were very light indeed. Indeed the division had taken heavier casualties in training on the night of 28 April, in Exercise 'Tiger' in the training area off Slapton Sands in Dorset, when E-boats from Cherbourg broke into the Task Force U exercise, sinking two LSTs and damaging a third. Of the 727 military and civilian casualties on that occasion (638 of them killed), 429 had been from 1st ESB.

The 101st Airborne Division's known losses for D-Day were 182 killed and 537 wounded, with 1,240 missing; 82nd Airborne Division's losses were 156 killed, 347 wounded and 756 missing, later assumed dead. These and the losses given above should be set against the strength of VII Corps on D-Day of 89,147 all ranks.

Dead American soldiers awaiting identification and burial not far from Ste-Mère-Église, 7 June. *(USNA)*

The last remaining episode of D-Day at Utah Beach was the German counter-attack from the south by 6th Paratroop Regiment. *Major* von der Heydte, commanding the regiment, reached St-Côme-du-Mont before 1100 hours, and drew up a plan for II/6th Paratroop Regiment to advance northwards along the main road towards Ste-Mère-Église, and I/6th Paratroop Regiment to advance north-eastwards towards Ste-Marie-du-Mont, leaving III/1058th Grenadiers dug in at St-Côme-du-Mont in reserve. Artillery support was planned from 4/191st and 8/191st Artillery Regiment plus a Flak battery from 243rd Infantry Division.

At 1330 hours Colonel Johnson of 501st PIR had begun his own advance from la Barquette west towards the main road bridge across the Douve south of St-Côme-du-Mont, bringing down fire on III/1058th Grenadiers, including some from the nine 8-inch guns of the cruiser USS *Quincy*. At 1730 hours, under

C-47 Skytrains towing Airspeed Horsa gliders carrying supplies fly over the former WN-5/WN-104 position on Utah Beach on the evening of D-Day. *(USNA)*

attack from Allied aircraft as they moved along the causeway road from Carentan and up the slope to the ridge, *Major* von der Heydte's men reached their forming-up points near St-Côme-du-Mont. With German resistance stiffening as 6th Paratroop Regiment began to arrive, Colonel Johnson and his men went on the defensive at about 2000 hours. Other groups of 501st PIR formed a rough line back to the hamlet of Angouville-au-Plain, south of the Ste-Marie-du-Mont road, leaving a gap between there and 8th Infantry's positions further north at les Forges.

At 1900 hours 6th Paratroop Regiment's counter-attack finally began, based on the orders issued by Seventh Army fifteen hours earlier. At first the German advance through the hedgerows made some progress in the face of American small arms and artillery, largely into the gap between 501st PIR and 8th Infantry. For a while Angouville-au-Plain was contested by both sides. At their furthest advance von der Heydte's battalions were level on either side of DZ C and LZ E when, at 2053 hours, 32 large Horsa gliders towed by C-47s began to land on LZ E, accompanied by supply parachute drops from more C-47s. These gliders carried 40 jeeps, 6 air-portable 75-mm guns, 19 tons of equipment and 157 members of 327th GIR; 44 men became casualties of the landing. A few minutes later, 54 Horsas and 22 Wacos carrying

64 jeeps, 13 air-portable 57-mm guns, medical and signals troops and 80th AAA Battalion for 82nd Airborne came down on LZ W, just north of the les Forges crossroads, which were still under German fire despite the efforts of Howell Force. One C-47 tug aircraft was hit 65 times but kept flying; 14 Wacos and 11 Horsas landed safely on the zone, many others close to it. But at least some gliders came down north-east of Ste-Mère-Église; the occupants were reached by American patrols that night.

Mayor Alexandre Renaud (in the back on the left, wearing a hat and light jacket) with the Simons family of Ste-Mère-Église, who are eating outdoors with two American soldiers after their home was damaged in the fighting, Photographed on 7 June. *(USNA)*

The attackers of 6th Paratroop Regiment over-estimated the number of gliders passing overhead, jumped to the conclusion that they were carrying infantry, and mistook supply bundles from the C-47s for paratroopers. Convinced that they were being surrounded, the Germans continued to report further major landings all around them throughout the night. At 2255 hours there was a final fly-in by 86 Horsas and 14 Wacos carrying 319th Field Artillery with 57-mm guns and 320th Field Artillery with 105-mm howitzers for 82nd Airborne Division, aiming for LZ W. Almost all the gliders found the landing zone successfully, losing 39 dead and 135 wounded, and 9 guns. At about the same time that this last wave of gliders arrived, the main artillery support for von der Heydte's advance, 4/191st Artillery Regiment, was hit by a devastating concentration of Allied naval gunfire. By then, men of I/6th Paratroop Regiment had fought to within sight of Ste-Marie-du-Mont and II/6th Paratroop Regiment to the nearby hamlet of Hiesville, some of its leading patrols perhaps as far as Ste-Mère-Église itself. But, trapped in the hedgerows by American firepower and increasingly cut off from their line of retreat to St-Côme-du-Mont, as D-Day ended the last German counter-attack stuttered to a halt.

CHAPTER 6

SECURING THE BEACHHEAD

The next battles fought by VII Corps were to secure its original D-Day objectives, including reaching 82nd Airborne Division at Ste-Mère-Église and linking-up with V Corps from Omaha Beach. The broad plan was for 4th Infantry Division to attack northwards to the le Ham–Montebourg–Quinéville ridge, 82nd Airborne Division to attack westward across the River Merderet, and 101st Airborne Division to attack southwards to capture Carentan. As a preliminary, on the evening of 6 June Maj Gen Taylor ordered Colonel Robert Sink commanding 506th PIR to assemble a task force including 528 men of his own 1/506th PIR and 2/506th PIR, reinforced by 1/401st GIR, to seize St-Côme-du-Mont and the causeway bridges through to Carentan. Next day, Lt Gen Bradley ordered V Corps and VII Corps to close the gap between themselves as a priority.

On the morning of 7 June the last glider lifts for 82nd Airborne took place, flying in from the west. At 0655 hours 18 Horsas and 82 Wacos in two groups landed 1/325th GIR with its regimental headquarters and some specialist troops on LZ E and LZ W for the loss of 17 men killed. At 0851 hours, in the final fly-in, 30 Horsas and 70 Wacos landed 2/325th GIR and 2/401st GIR (officially designated 3/325th GIR but also often given its older title) on LZ W for the loss of 18 killed. In the two landings, 68 men were also seriously injured and 57 slightly injured. As before, some of the gliders landed on the designated zones, but others landed elsewhere along the main Cherbourg road or in the

HISTORY

Merderet swamps. The 101st Airborne Division's glider regiment, 327th GIR, came ashore at Utah Beach, together with more troops of 90th Infantry Division. In the course of 7 June American firepower succeeded in knocking out or suppressing most of the German artillery firing onto Utah Beach.

On the German side, higher level headquarters continued to believe that the Utah beachhead (or, as they thought of it, the Ste-Mère-Église pocket) was the most important sector of the landings, based on their assessment that the main American objective was Cherbourg, and that the gap across the Vire estuary made Utah Beach vulnerable. By 8 June captured Allied documents had revealed First Army's plan for linking up Omaha and Utah beaches, and in response Rommel wanted to use any arriving German reserves to drive into the Cotentin and destroy VII Corps before this could happen. He was over-ruled by Hitler and OKW, who were convinced that Cherbourg could be defended indefinitely, and that the forces already in the Cotentin (three divisions and a brigade) should be enough to hold the Americans. Rommel repeated his views on 11 June, arguing unsuccessfully for the armoured divisions by then opposing Second (British) Army far to the east at Caen to be relieved by infantry and sent to the Cotentin.

A typical improvised German strongpoint immediately inland from the landings at Utah Beach, based on a cottage or farm building. Photographed on 11 June. *(USNA)*

In fact, although Lt Gen Bradley in particular favoured an early capture of Cherbourg, the Allies had always planned to land their troops and supplies across the beaches for as long as necessary. Shortly after mid-day on 7 June at Utah (as at the other landing beaches) they began to sink obsolete merchant ships out to sea to form a breakwater code-named 'Gooseberry' providing a sheltered anchorage; altogether ten American merchant ships totalling 57,148 gross tons were sunk in this way by 10 June. When bad weather a few days later caused delays in landing, the gentle shelving beach at Utah also proved excellent for the expedient of 'drying out' landing craft and even the much larger LSTs by deliberately beaching them to unload their cargo

An American command post on Utah Beach on 7 June. The sign reads 'Red Beach HQ'. *(USNA)*

and letting them float off again at high tide. By 12 June, 1,000 metres of the original planned Utah Beach at les Dunes de Varreville, now designated Roger White beach, had been cleared of obstacles. This became the main landing and unloading beach at Utah for the rest of the campaign.

For the resumption of the German attack southwards from Montebourg towards Ste-Mère-Église on 7 June, 1058th Grenadiers and 7th Assault Battalion were reinforced by 456th and 457th Artillery Battalions (both motorised with twelve medium and heavy guns each, although on the journey southwards 456th Artillery had been badly mauled in an ambush by American paratroopers) and the assault company of 709th Anti-Tank Battalion. In addition, III/729th Grenadiers advanced southwards to the east of Montebourg, and 243rd Infantry Division contributed Battlegroup *Müller*: III/922nd Grenadiers (with regimental attachments), I/920th Grenadiers, and 243rd Engineer Battalion, supported by III/243rd Artillery Regiment (less one battery). Also joining the forces on the Montebourg ridge was 101st Fortress Rocket Projector Regiment, a motorised unit of three battalions with 54 *Nebelwerfer* rocket launchers, known to the Allies as 'Screaming Mimis' or 'Moaning Minnies' from their distinctive sound. At least one battery of this regiment had been present near Ste-Marie-du-Mont on D-Day.

HISTORY

On the American side, the first priority for 8th Infantry on 7 June was to eliminate 795th Georgian Battalion in its pocket south of Ste-Mère-Église. Starting late in the morning, 1/8th Infantry attacked the Georgians from the east while 2/8th and 3/8th Infantry swung up northwards from les Forges. At this critical time, a Russian-speaking sergeant of 4th Infantry Division, who had been taken prisoner by the Georgians, convinced a group of 75 men to surrender, and altogether the battalion capitulated with 174 men just as 1/8th Infantry entered Turqueville.

American infantry with heavy weapons moving up through the hedgerows inland from Utah Beach on 8 June. *(USNA)*

Earlier in the morning, with artillery support I/1058th Grenadiers and II/1058th Grenadiers had renewed their attack southwards on both sides of the main Cherbourg road towards Ste-Mère-Église, with 7th Assault Battalion joining in to the east and III/922nd Grenadiers of Battlegroup *Müller* attacking towards St-Marcouf. At first the attack against 2/505th PIR went well. Then tanks from 746th Tank Battalion of 4th Infantry Division from Utah Beach counter-attacked from the east, swinging north of Ste-Mère-Église. In the narrow lanes and hedgerows these tanks struck one German column, led by five assault guns of 709th Anti-Tank Battalion, forcing them to retreat. Even so, in the early afternoon troops of 1058th Grenadiers broke into the northern part of Ste-Mère-Église, and for a brief moment, LXXXIV Corps recorded (wrongly) that the town was again in German hands. Following the surrender of 795th Georgian Battalion, 2/8th Infantry and tanks of 70th Tank Battalion were rushed to Ste-Mère-Église and at once committed alongside 2/505th PIR in fighting off 1058th Grenadiers' attack from the north-west. By nightfall the Americans had taken 300 prisoners and secured the north-western sector of the Ste-Mère-Église defences. The tanks of 746th Tank Battalion pressed on as far north as Neuville-au-Plain, where they remained until 2100 hours before withdrawing southwards. Meanwhile the three battalions of 325th GIR that had landed that morning assembled near les Forges to replace 8th Infantry, and then pushed westward to reach Chef-du-Pont at 1615 hours, substantially reinforcing the American position there.

American paratroopers beside a churchyard near St-Marcouf on 8 June. *(USNA)*

East of the main Cherbourg road, the German attack from the north also went well at first. Advancing alongside 1058th Grenadiers, at least some troops of 7th Assault Battalion got as far as the church and main square at Ste-Mère-Église, even linking up with soldiers from 795th Georgian Battalion. But in the course of the day this attack was driven back by 2/12th Infantry and 1/12th Infantry, continuing their own drive northward, supported by 899th Tank Destroyer Battalion, with 3/12th Infantry in reserve and 2/22nd and 1/22nd Infantry on their right.

The two casemated batteries at Azeville and Crisbecq now functioned as small fortresses for the Germans against these American attacks from the south, and as a rallying point for the troops from 919th Grenadiers escaping from the Utah Beach area. Most of 7th Assault Battalion fell back north-east towards the Azeville battery, which was unsuccessfully attacked by 2/22nd Infantry later in the day. In a last German attack from the north on 7 June, III/922nd Grenadiers advanced past the Crisbecq battery as far south as St-Marcouf before being driven back north again, although a follow-up attempt by 1/22nd Infantry to take the Crisbecq battery was repulsed by 1600 hours, with the Azeville battery firing in its support onto the American attackers.

American soldiers entering St-Marcouf village, just south of the Crisbecq battery, on 8 June. (USNA)

Only four of the resistance nests and strongpoints from Exit 4 northwards defended by I/919th Grenadiers (referred to by the Americans as WN-10, WN-10a, WN-11 and S-12) were still holding out during 7 June, otherwise 3/22nd Infantry continued to clear the beach areas by advancing up the coast. The Germans

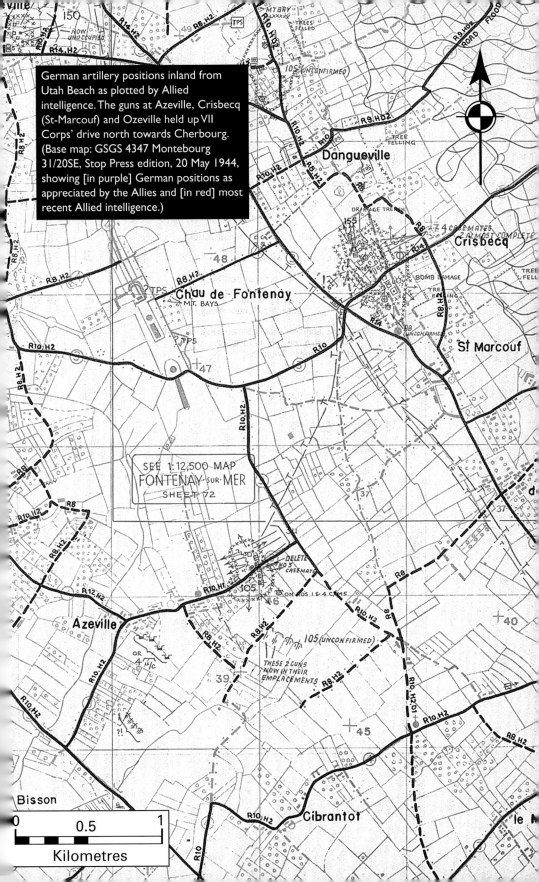

German artillery positions inland from Utah Beach as plotted by Allied intelligence. The guns at Azeville, Crisbecq (St-Marcouf) and Ozeville held up VII Corps' drive north towards Cherbourg. (Base map: GSGS 4347 Montebourg 31/20SE, Stop Press edition, 20 May 1944, showing [in purple] German positions as appreciated by the Allies and [in red] most recent Allied intelligence.)

found any movement close to the shore extremely difficult due to the guns of the Allied warships, making it impossible for their northern counter-attack to develop any momentum. By late afternoon, GenLt von Schlieben had decided that his local reserves were insufficient to eliminate the American beachhead, and ordered his 709th Infantry Division onto the defensive, bringing the last of his troops down from the north except for a few skeleton crews. The composition of the improvised German battlegroups could change daily, but broadly the defensive line to the north against 4th Infantry Division consisted of I/1058th and II/1058th Grenadiers holding the line north of Neuville-au-Plain, then Battlegroup *Rohrbach* (chiefly elements of 729th Grenadiers but including II/920th Grenadiers) to the coastal ridge road at Fontenay-sur-Mer, then Battlegroup *Keil* (including III/922nd Grenadiers and III/739th Grenadiers), and finally Battlegroup *Müller* prolonging the line to the coast.

To the west, after repeated but unsuccessful attempts throughout 7 June by 1057th Grenadiers to force the la Fière causeway against 1/505th PIR, 91st Airlanding Division also went onto the defensive, holding the German line from le Ham through to Carentan. In the late evening, 82nd Airborne Division redeployed its glider regiment from Chef-du-Pont, sending 1/325th GIR to la Fière and 2/325th GIR to Ste-Mère-Église. After dark on 8 June, troops of 1/325th GIR crossed the floods of the Merderet by a submerged pathway north of la Fière to link up with Lt Col Timmes' group of 2/507th PIR near Amfreville. At 1045 hours on 9 June, 3/325th (2/401st) GIR and tanks of 746th Tank Battalion attacked across the la Fière causeway after a 15-minute bombardment, including fire from 155-mm guns of the newly arrived 90th Infantry Division. By this time the defenders of 1057th Grenadiers at Cauquigny were probably no more than two weak companies. After an epic fight along the causeway and in the hedgerows, by shortly after 1200 hours the glider troops, joined by a company of 507th PIR, were beyond Cauquigny in force. By 1545 hours, troops from 1/508th PIR had also crossed the causeway and linked up with Lt Col Shanley's group at Hill 30, and by nightfall the west bank of the Merderet was at last secure for the Americans.

In the fighting to the end of 9 June 1/325th GIR and 3/325th GIR had lost 60 dead, 238 wounded and 246 missing including many drowned, or almost half their combined rifle strength.

Amphibious vehicles of 470th Amphibious Truck Company, part of 1st Engineer Special Brigade, continuing to land stores and supplies at Utah Beach on 8 June. (USNA)

Early on 10 June, troops of 2/357th Infantry crossed the la Fière causeway as part of the planned relief of 82nd Airborne Division by 90th Infantry Division. This was the start of First Army's plan for the next phase of the battle, the attack westward by 90th Infantry Division to cut the Cotentin peninsula leading to the capture of Cherbourg.

On the German side, on 11 June the first troops of 77th Infantry Division (10,505 strong – including 1,410 'volunteers' from eastern Europe – with only two infantry regiments) arrived from Brittany to support 91st Airlanding Division, deploying two battalions of 1049th Grenadiers to the north-west of the Ste-Mère-Église pocket and two battalions of 1050th Grenadiers to the west. In the fighting since D-Day, 91st Airlanding Division had reported losses of 2,212 troops.

To the south of Ste-Mère-Église, at daybreak on 7 June the two battalions of 6th Paratroop Regiment were still trapped in the hedgerows between the main Cherbourg road and Ste-Marie-du-Mont after their failed attack of the previous evening. At 0400 hours, Colonel Sink's advance towards St-Côme-du-Mont began, supported by tanks of 746th Tank Battalion. At 0630 hours, under attack from Allied fighter-bombers and artillery, the two battalions of 6th Paratroop Regiment were ordered to retreat. Disorganised columns of I/6th Paratroop Regiment, hoping to escape across the River Taute, ran into the isolated groups of 3/506th PIR holding the bridges at le Port and la Barquette lock. Despite their superiority in numbers, caught by surprise and arriving piecemeal, over 600 men of I/6th Paratroop Regiment had surrendered by nightfall, and only 25 survivors reached safety at Carentan. Next day 327th GIR took over the defence of la Barquette and le Port from the American paratroopers.

On 8 June at 0445 hours Colonel Sink renewed his attack from Angouville-au-Plain with four battalions – 1/506th PIR, 2/506th PIR, 3/501st PIR and 1/401st GIR – supported by artillery and naval gunnery. Blasted by the shellfire, III/1058th Grenadiers fell back from St-Côme-du-Mont together with most of II/6th Paratroop Regiment. Cutting the road south to Carentan, 3/501st PIR held off repeated attempts by the Germans to force their way through. Instead, most of the Germans found alternate routes westward into the marshes and then southwards along the railway line. By this time most of the Americans had been without proper sleep or rest since late on 5 June, and the German retreat to Carentan was not strongly pursued. The 101st Airborne was also still largely dependent on naval gunnery and on 65th and 87th Armored Field Artillery. Its own 377th Parachute Field Artillery was still reassembling after the D-Day drop, while the steamer SS *Susan B. Anthony* with the crews of 321st Glider Field Artillery had struck a mine and sunk off Utah Beach on D-Day, and delays in landing meant that it was not until 10 June that the battalion came into action, together with 907th Glider Field Artillery.

Perhaps deceived by optimistic reports on 7 June, OB West continued to believe that there was still a real chance of encircling and destroying the Americans at Ste-Mère-Église. Even by 8 June, LXXXIV Corps' assessment was that they had thwarted the Allied plan to capture Cherbourg quickly, and that they could hold the beachhead to the north and west for some time. But General Marcks urgently demanded more artillery and infantry anti-tank weapons from Seventh Army. Five more batteries of 1261st and 1262nd Coastal Artillery were redeployed to support the Montebourg–Quinéville line, and the long range 170-mm guns of 10/1261st Coastal Artillery from the west coast began shelling Utah Beach from 30 km away; 91st Airlanding Division (which was no longer able to get ammunition for its own artillery) was re-equipped with new guns.

Men of the 101st Airborne Division in St-Marcouf on 8 June. *(USNA)*

Despite the massive Allied superiority at sea, the E-boats from Cherbourg continued to come out at night, concentrating on minelaying and raids on Allied traffic across the Channel. On 7 June off Utah Beach the minesweeper USS *Tide* was sunk by a mine; on 8 June the destroyers USS *Glennon*, USS *Meredith* and USS *Rich* were sunk by mines together with the netlayer HMS *Minister* and the motor minesweepers MSS 229 and YMS 406; and on 12 June an E-boat from Cherbourg torpedoed the destroyer USS *Nelson*.

There was still little impact on the battle from the German Air Force. With nightfall on D-Day, six RAF Mosquito night fighter squadrons took over the role of fighter protection over the Normandy beachheads. The level of fighter cover by day or night was gradually reduced after 11 June as it became clear that there was little German air threat. On 8 June, 819th Aviation Engineering Battalion built an emergency grass landing strip at

Pouppeville, and another followed at la Londe Farm north-east of Ste-Mère-Église on 11 June. In contrast, the constant threat from Allied aircraft greatly affected every German movement. On 9 June GenLt von Schlieben was strafed by two USAAF P-47 Thunderbolts while driving to one of his units, and had to walk the rest of the way from his burning car.

Meanwhile, the American drive north from Ste-Mère-Église to the coast continued. On 8 June 12th Infantry attacked east of the main Cherbourg road, with 8th Infantry to the west, supported by 2/325th GIR and 3/505th PIR even further west to the line of the Merderet. As the depleted German battlegroups were worn down, the main strength of their defence came from the hedgerow country itself and from the guns and rockets of 456th and 457th Artillery Battalions, III/243rd Artillery Regiment and 101st Fortress Rocket Projector Regiment (including the improvised 'Artillery Group Montebourg' of nineteen guns from five different batteries). By 12 June, 4th Infantry Division had largely reached the le Ham–Montebourg–Quinéville road, slightly to the north of its original D-Day objectives, and was ordered to dig in and hold.

On the eastern flank, 4th Infantry Division repeated its attempts to take the Azeville and Crisbecq Batteries on 8 June. After a 20-minute bombardment by mortars, artillery and naval gunnery, 2/22nd Infantry again attacked the Azeville battery, which continued to hold out and again to give supporting fire to the Crisbecq battery, enabling it to repulse an attack by 1/22nd Infantry Regiment. On 9 June, 44th Field Artillery Battalion fired 1,500 rounds at the Azeville battery before 3/22nd Infantry (supported by one Sherman tank) finally captured it using bazooka anti-tank launchers, flame throwers, and satchel charges. The Americans decided to by-pass the Crisbecq battery and push on, leaving it masked by infantry and tank destroyers.

In the late afternoon of 9 June OKW ordered OB West to move all available supplies into Cherbourg, and Field Marshal von Rundstedt issued his own orders that demolition of Cherbourg docks should start. Almost the last German reserves in the Cotentin, two further battalions from 243rd Infantry Division, II/921st Grenadiers and I/922nd Grenadiers, were ordered to move from Cherbourg to join 91st Airlanding Division. On 10 June GenLt von Schlieben added a final reserve to the defences of Montebourg, 20 French-built tanks with

Then: One of the 105-mm gun casemates of the Azeville battery, photographed on 15 June 1944. *(USNA)*

Now: A modern view of the former 105-mm casemate at the Azeville battery. *(Author)*

Then: One of the casemated 210-mm guns of the Crisbecq battery after its capture by American troops. Photographed on 21 June. *(USNA)*

Now: One of the Crisbecq battery casemates today. *(Author)*

37-mm guns. Since 8 June his own depleted 709th Infantry Division had been recorded by Seventh Army as Battlegroup *Schlieben*. General Marcks considered 10 June to be the last day on which the American beachhead at Utah was still weak enough to be successfully contained. As the Americans attacked northwards and westwards from the Utah beachhead, LXXXIV Corps transferred command of the forces engaged around Utah Beach from Quinéville round to Carentan to the commander of 243rd Infantry Division as Battlegroup *Hellmich*.

After nightfall on 11 June the garrison of the Crisbecq battery was ordered to escape northward, and at 0820 hours on 12 June, American troops of 2/39th Infantry, from the newly arrived 9th Infantry Division, came forward to find only 21 wounded with a medical orderly left behind. Two days later, 3/39th Infantry, attacking in conjunction with 22nd Infantry, captured Quinéville, a final D-Day objective. The arrival of 9th Infantry Division as well as 90th Infantry Division meant that VII Corps was now strong enough for its planned advance to Cherbourg.

CHAPTER 7

THE CAPTURE OF CARENTAN

While 4th Infantry Division and 82nd Airborne Divisions were securing their objectives to the north and west, there remained the need to link up with V Corps from Omaha Beach. On 8 June, Maj Gen Taylor, commanding 101st Airborne Division, reported to Maj Gen Collins that St-Côme-du-Mont was secure. Collins duly conferred with Lt Gen Bradley, whose First Army headquarters was now ashore just inland of Omaha Beach, and Taylor was ordered to take Carentan next. Since a large gap had been blown in the Cherbourg railway embankment that route could not be used, so the only direct approach was down the slope from St-Côme-du-Mont and along the exposed causeway carrying the main road. This route was barely ten metres wide with virtually no cover and little hard ground on either side, across four damaged or destroyed bridges over the minor River

Jourdan, the River Douve, and the minor River Groult and River Madeleine.

On the German side, on 9 June patrols from II/6th Paratroop Regiment from Carentan found no other German troops between themselves and the River Vire to the east. Instead, stragglers from units intended to defend the estuary were falling back into Carentan as V Corps advanced from Omaha Beach. LXXXIV Corps transferred these troops, including two *Ost* battalions, to 6th Paratroop Regiment, and these were used to cover the eastern side of Carentan while III/6th and II/6th Paratroop Regiment took up positions supported by one 88-mm battery facing north-west on either side of the causeway road.

An aerial view of the centre of Carentan, including the church. The flat lands of the Vire Estuary and the rising ground beyond leading to Utah Beach are visible in the distance. Photograph taken from 400 feet on 4 July. *(USNA)*

The attack by 101st Airborne Division to take Carentan began in the early hours of 10 June, after reconnaissance had suggested the town might be lightly held. The plan was for 327th GIR to outflank Carentan from the north across the River Taute while 502nd PIR pushed directly down the causeway from St-Côme-du-Mont. At 0145 hours, after a brief artillery and mortar bombardment, 1/327th GIR began its crossing of the Taute. By 0600 hours all three glider battalions were across and had captured Brévands, with the double intention of pushing east to link up with V Corps, which had reached Isigny-sur-Mer on the far side of the Vire estuary, and circling round Carentan from the north. Through the afternoon 1/401st GIR pressed eastward in a running fight with German troops who were falling back westwards to Carentan. Its lead company reached the hamlet of Auville-sur-le-Vey (part of les Veys) just west of the River Vire, making the first contact with men of 29th Reconnaissance Troop and 175th Infantry from Omaha Beach. The other battalions of 327th GIR moved round to the east of Carentan and the Taute before coming under heavy German fire at 1800 hours.

Intermittent German shelling of Utah Beach continuing on 11 June. *(USNA)*

Meanwhile, at 0015 hours, 3/502nd PIR, led by troops of 326th Airborne Engineer Battalion to repair the bridges, had begun to move south-east along the causeway road towards Carentan. The leading patrols got as far as the final bridge over the River Madeleine, which was blocked by a Belgian Gate, before coming under fire and falling back shortly after dawn. The advance was resumed in the early afternoon with artillery support chiefly from 65th Armored Field Artillery and the recently arrived 907th Glider Field Artillery. Difficulties in repairing and crossing the bridges, and the road block at the Madeleine bridge, meant that the battalion had become strung out on the exposed causeway when, at about 1600 hours, the defenders of III/6th

Paratroop Regiment opened heavy fire from the hedgerows and a nearby farmhouse, supported by the 88-mm battery. The Americans were pinned in place, barely able to move, and only their own artillery prevented much heavier casualties. At 1800 hours one or two German aircraft bombed and strafed the causeway almost wiping out one American company, which was reduced to 23 officers and men. The paratroopers spent a dangerous night on the causeway, but gradually their two remaining companies (numbering only 60 and 84 men respectively) squeezed forward through the bridge roadblock before dawn.

Both sides were now in great difficulties. There was just about space on either side of the road for the Americans to move or to dig themselves in on the causeway and still be clear of the marsh. However, by the evening of 10 June, the defenders of Carentan were running low on ammunition, despite a supply drop by Junkers 52 and Heinkel 111 aircraft. By midnight, 1/327th GIR and 2/327th GIR had fought their way across the Taute and brought the centre of Carentan under fire from the north and east. At 1000 hours next morning troops of 2/327th GIR and 1/401st GIR renewed their attack south-westward, being stopped on the northern outskirts of the town.

American airborne troops in the streets of Carentan on 12 June. *(USNA)*

On the causeway road, at 0615 hours on 11 June after a 45-minute artillery bombardment, men of 3/502nd PIR charged forward under cover of a smokescreen against the German positions in the hedgerows and farmhouse buildings, with 1/502nd PIR coming up to reinforce them. It was a chaotic battle on both sides, often hand to hand. At noon, with so many dead and wounded, a one-hour medical truce was arranged. Maj Gen Taylor also sent a message to the Germans giving them the chance to surrender, but *Major* von der Heydte (who had been ordered by Hitler on 9 June to defend Carentan to the last man and bullet) rejected the suggestion. In the face of German counter-attacks and heavy losses, at 1830 hours 3/502nd PIR began to withdraw back along the causeway under cover of artillery and mortar fire. Of 640 men who had begun the attack, only 132 made it back to St-Côme-du-Mont, many of them wounded. Lt Col Cole commanding 3/502nd PIR was awarded the Medal of Honor for this battle. The other battalions of 502nd PIR also withdrew, to be replaced by 506th PIR.

The remaining defenders of Carentan were largely out of ammunition, and late in the afternoon *Major* von der Heydte gave orders to abandon the town. First the German troops to the east, including the two *Ost* battalions, and then the survivors of 6th Paratroop Regiment, began pulling back during the night, taking up new positions to the south-west including Hill 30. Throughout the night American artillery, naval guns, mortars and tank destroyers fired at the German positions in Carentan, setting the town on fire. At 0200 hours on 12 June, 506th PIR attacked from the bridgehead across the River Madeleine moving southwards to encircle the town with 502nd PIR in support. These troops linked up with 327th GIR who attacked from the north at 0600 hours, and 501st PIR which had also come across the River Taute at Brévands, attacking from the east. The American encircling movement liberated the town but failed to catch most of its defenders, who had already retreated. Pressing southwards, 1/506th PIR drove the Russian 439th *Ost* Battalion off Hill 30. In the afternoon 1/327th GIR and 2/327th GIR were sent with some tank destroyers eastward to the River Vire to strengthen the link with V Corps from Omaha. Meanwhile 501st PIR pushed forward a short distance south-west of Hill 30 with 506th PIR to its west covering the River Douve.

While this was happening, the leading elements of 17th SS

The D-Day landing site at Utah Beach, looking north along the coast. Photographed on 2 August. *(USNA)*

Panzergrenadier Division *Götz von Berlichingen* under *SS-Gruppenführer* (Maj-Gen) Werner Ostendorff arrived to reinforce the defence of Carentan. The division's journey to the front, which had started on 7 June, had been greatly delayed by lack of fuel and transport, and by Allied air attacks. The German commanders blamed each other for Carentan's abandonment, and planned a counter-attack next day. That morning, General Marcks drove forward from LXXXIV Corps headquarters at St-Lô to confer with his commanders as far away as Quinéville. After stopping near Carentan he drove off towards St-Lô; on this road his car was strafed by Allied aircraft, and he was killed.

The German plan for 13 June was for III/6th Paratroop Regiment to recapture Hill 30, while II/6th Paratroop Regiment with troops of 37th and 38th SS Panzergrenadier Regiments led by 17th SS Assault Gun Battalion drove in a surprise attack without artillery preparation into the gap to the west between Carentan and the River Douve, turning to attack the town from the north-west. The attack began at 0700 hours, and for two hours there was no contact with the Americans until the leading Germans reached to within 500 metres of the town. There they were met by 2/502nd PIR moving up from reserve, together with Combat Command A (commanded by Colonel John H. Collier) of 2nd Armored Division, coming across from V Corps,

American paratroopers holding a captured German flag on 8 June. *(USNA)*

supported by 14th Armored Field Artillery Battalion. By noon the German advance had been halted, and by 1400 hours the Americans had begun to drive them back south-west of Carentan. At the same time news came through of the start of a new American attack westwards out of the Merderet–Douve bridgehead, threatening the northern flank of any future German attack. Carentan and the junction between Utah and Omaha Beaches were now secure.

Hitler's response to the fall of Carentan was to send an edict on 12 June to all commanders in Normandy that 'no orders for retreat will be issued' and that commanders must tell their men to defend each position to the last. Hitler also ordered the Allied beachheads to be eliminated, starting with the British Sword Beach to the east at Caen and progressing westwards to Utah Beach. These decisions would give the rest of the Battle of Normandy much of its shape for the next month. But in the Cotentin one phase of the battle was at an end, and both sides were briefly drawing breath. For VII Corps, a firm junction with the forces from Omaha Beach, a solid line to the north facing the Montebourg–Quinéville ridge, and increasing pressure towards the west out of the Merderet–Douve bridgehead, all meant that the fight for Utah Beach was successfully over.

PART THREE

BATTLEFIELD TOURS

GENERAL TOURING INFORMATION

Normandy is a thriving holiday area, with some beautiful countryside, excellent beaches and very attractive architecture (particularly in the case of religious buildings). It was also, of course, the scene of heavy fighting in 1944, and this has had a considerable impact on the tourist industry. To make the most of your trip, especially if you intend visiting non-battlefield sites, we strongly recommend you purchase one of the general Normandy guidebooks that are commonly available. These include: *Michelin Green Guide: Normandy*; *Thomas Cook Travellers: Normandy*; *The Rough Guide to Brittany and Normandy*; *Lonely Planet: Normandy*.

TRAVEL REQUIREMENTS

First, make sure you have the proper documentation to enter France as a tourist. Citizens of European Union countries, including Great Britain, should not usually require visas, but will need to carry and show their passports. Others should check with the French Embassy in their own country before travelling. British citizens should also fill in and take Form E111 (available from main post offices), which deals with entitlement to medical treatment, and all should consider taking out comprehensive travel insurance. France is part of the Eurozone, and you should also check exchange rates before travelling.

GETTING THERE

The most direct routes from the UK to Lower Normandy are by ferry from Portsmouth to Ouistreham (near Caen), and from Portsmouth or Poole to Cherbourg. Depending on which you choose, and whether you travel by day or night, the crossing takes between five and seven hours. Alternatively, you can sail to Le Havre, Boulogne or Calais and drive the rest of the way. (Travel time from Calais to Caen is about four hours; motorway and bridge tolls may be payable depending on the exact route taken.) Another option is to use the Channel Tunnel. Whichever way you travel, early booking is advised, especially in summer.

Although you can of course hire motor vehicles in Normandy, the majority of visitors from the UK or other EU countries will probably take their own. If you do so, you will also need to take: a full driving licence; your vehicle registration document; a certificate of motor insurance valid in France (your insurer will advise on this); spare headlight and indicator bulbs; headlight beam adjusters or tape; a warning triangle; and a sticker or number plate identifying which country the vehicle is registered in. Visitors from elsewhere should consult a motoring organisation in their home country for details of the documents and other items they will require.

Above: One of the 210-mm casemates of the Crisbecq battery, showing the effects of demolition by US Engineers. *(Author)*

Page 111: Some Americans commandeered horses to get around the hedgerow country. These paratroopers were seen in Ste-Mère-Église, on 8 June. *(USNA)*

The Normandy road system is well developed, although there are still a few choke points, especially around the larger towns during rush hour and in the holiday season. As a general guide, in clear conditions it is possible to drive from Cherbourg to Caen in less than two hours.

ACCOMMODATION

Accommodation in Normandy is plentiful and diverse, from cheap campsites to five star hotels in glorious châteaux. However,

The Cotentin peninsula in 1944. This picture shows the coast at Vauville, on the north-western part of the peninsula, looking south and showing the Atlantic Wall beach defences. *(USNA)*

early booking is advised if you wish to travel between June and August. Useful contacts include:

French Travel Centre, 178 Piccadilly, London W1V 0AL;
  tel: 0870 830 2000; web: www.raileurope.co.uk
Calvados Tourisme, Place du Canada, 14000 Caen;
  tel: +33 (0)2 31 86 53 30; web: www.calvados-tourisme.com
Manche Tourisme; web: www.manchetourisme.com
Maison du Tourisme de Cherbourg et du Haut-Cotentin,
  2 Quai Alexandre III, 50100 Cherbourg-Octeville;
  tel: +33 (0)2 33 93 52 02; web: www.ot-cherbourg-cotentin.fr
Gîtes de France, La Maison des Gîtes de France et du Tourisme
  Vert, 59 rue Saint-Lazare, 75 439 Paris Cedex 09;
  tel: +33 (0)1 49 70 75 75; web: www.gites-de-france.fr

BATTLEFIELD TOURING

Each volume in the 'Battle Zone Normandy' series contains from four to six battlefield tours. These are intended to last from a few hours to a full day apiece. Some are best undertaken using motor transport, others should be done on foot, and many involve a mixture of the two. Owing to its excellent infrastructure and relatively gentle topography, Normandy also makes a good location for a cycling holiday; indeed, some of our tours are ideally suited to this method.

In every case the tour author has visited the area concerned recently, so the information presented should be accurate and reasonably up to date. Nevertheless land use, infrastructure and rights of way can change, sometimes at short notice. If you encounter difficulties in following any tour, we would very much like to hear about it, so we can incorporate changes in future editions. Your comments should be sent to the publisher at the address provided at the front of this book.

To derive maximum value and enjoyment from the tours, we suggest you equip yourself with the following items:

- Appropriate maps. European road atlases can be purchased from a wide range of locations outside France. However, for navigation within Normandy, the French Institut Géographique National (IGN <www.ign.fr>) produces maps at a variety of scales. The 1:100,000 series ('Top 100') is particularly useful when driving over larger distances; sheet 06 (Caen – Cherbourg) covers most of the invasion area. For pinpointing locations precisely, the current IGN 1:25,000 Série Bleue is best (we use extracts from this series for the tour maps in this book). These can be purchased in many places across Normandy. They can also be ordered in the UK from some bookshops, or from specialist dealers such as the Hereford Map Centre, 24–25 Church Street, Hereford HR1 2LR; tel: 01432 266322; web: <www.themapcentre.com>. Allow at least a fortnight's notice, although some maps may be in stock.
- Lightweight waterproof clothing and robust footwear are essential, especially for touring in the countryside.
- Take a compass, provided you know how to use one!
- A camera and spare films/memory cards.
- A notebook and writing materials to record what you have photographed.

- A French dictionary and/or phrasebook. (English is widely spoken in the coastal area, but is much less common inland.)
- Food and drink. Although you are never very far in Normandy from a shop, restaurant or *tabac*, many of the tours do not pass directly by such facilities. It is therefore sensible to take some light refreshment with you.
- Binoculars. Most officers and some other ranks carried binoculars in 1944. Taking a pair adds a surprising amount of verisimilitude to the touring experience.

A typical Normandy farmhouse barn and walled farmyard. This example shows signs of repair to the stonework since 1944. *(Author)*

SOME DO'S AND DON'TS

Battlefield touring can be an extremely interesting and even emotional experience, especially if you have read something about the battles beforehand. In addition, it is fair to say that residents of Normandy are used to visitors, among them battlefield tourists, and generally will do their best to help if you encounter problems. However, many of the tours in the 'Battle Zone Normandy' series are off the beaten track, and you can expect some puzzled looks from the locals, especially inland. In all cases care has been taken to ensure that tours are on public land, or viewable from public rights of way. In the unlikely event that you are asked to leave a site, do so immediately and by the most direct route.

In addition: **Never remove 'souvenirs' from the battlefields.** Even today it is not unknown for farmers to turn up relics of the

1944 fighting. Taking these without permission may not only be illegal, but can be extremely dangerous. It also ruins the site for genuine battlefield archaeologists. Anyone returning from France should also remember customs regulations on the import of weapons and ammunition of any kind.

Be especially careful when investigating fortifications. Some of the more frequently-visited sites are well preserved, and several of them have excellent museums. However, both along the coast and inland, there are numerous positions that have been left to decay, and which carry risks for the unwary. In particular, remember that many of these places were the scenes of heavy fighting or subsequent demolitions, which may have caused severe (and sometimes invisible) structural damage. Coastal erosion has also undermined the foundations of a number of shoreline defences. Under no circumstances should underground bunkers, chambers and tunnels be entered, and care should always be taken when examining above-ground structures. If in any doubt, stay away.

A modern view of the western edge of Chef-du-Pont village, which has expanded considerably since 1944, looking back east along the D70 from close to the US Airborne Memorial Gardens. *(Author)*

Beware of hunting (shooting) areas (signposted *Chasse Gardée*). Do not enter these, even if they offer a short cut to your destination. Similarly, Normandy contains a number of restricted areas (military facilities and wildlife reserves), which should be avoided. Watch out, too, for temporary footpath closures, especially along sections of coastal cliffs.

If using a motor vehicle, keep your eyes on the road. There are many places to park, even on minor routes, and it is always better to turn round and retrace your path than to cause an accident. In rural areas avoid blocking entrances and driving along farm tracks; again, it is better to walk a few hundred metres than to cause damage and offence.

NON-MILITARY ATTRACTIONS

In addition to the battlefields, one of the great charms of Normandy is that it is a holiday and tourist centre in its own right. The former battlefields of Utah Beach and the Ste-Mère-Église area are only a short drive from many places of non-military interest, either north towards Cherbourg or east towards Bayeux and Caen. Many of these are mentioned in other volumes in the 'Battle Zone Normandy' series. Within the region covered by this book, the two main attractions are the coastline and the beach itself, and the Regional Nature Reserve of the Cotentin and Bessin Marshland Park, which covers much of the inland area.

Useful Local Contacts

Carentan Office de Tourisme, Boulevard de Verdun – BP 204, 50500 Carentan; tel: +33 (0)2 33 71 23 50; web: <www.ot-carentan.fr>; email: <info@ot-carentan.fr>.

Montebourg Office de Tourisme, 20, Rue du Général Leclerc, 50310 Montebourg; tel: +33 (0)2 33 41 15 73; web: <www.tourisme.fr/office-de-tourisme/montebourg.htm>.

Ste-Mère-Église Office de Tourisme, 6, Rue Eisenhower, 50480 Ste-Mère-Église; tel: +33 (0)2 33 21 00 33; web: <www.sainte-mere-eglise.info; email: <bienvenue@sainte-mere-eglise.info>.

Les Ponts d'Ouve Visitor Centre, Espace de découverte des Marais du Cotentin et du Bessin, 50500 St-Côme-du-Mont; tel: +33 (0)2 33 71 65 30; web: <www.parc-cotentin-bessin.fr/ponts_douve/frset_ponts.htm>; email: <ponts.douve@wanadoo.fr>.

Cotentin Farm Museum, Chemin de Beauvais, 50480 Ste-Mère-Église; tel: +33 (0)2 33 95 40 20.

Utah-Beach Camping, Régine Cardet, 50480 Ste-Marie-du-Mont.

The attractive sand beach with its wild dunes is continuous from Quinéville (which also has a marina for boats) southwards to the Utah Beach memorials, and its gentle shelving makes it very appealing to families. Any of the small villages in the area provide basic facilities for a quiet seaside holiday. Architecturally, many of the churches are worth visiting for their own sake, including that in Ste-Mère-Église itself, Beuzeville-au-Plain, Ste-Marie-du-Mont with its unusual tower, and St-Côme-du-Mont which dates from the 12th century. A description of the architectural features of the villages in the region, including their churches, can be found at <www.welcome.sainte-mere-eglise.info/stemere/html/eng/heritage/architecture.html>.

The view from Utah Beach inland over the drained pastureland, flooded in 1944, looking towards the coastal ridge with its church spires and road. *(Author)*

The only nightclub listed in the area is *Le Moulin Normand* at Quinéville, and anyone looking for exciting night-life should base themselves in another part of Normandy.

Ste-Mère-Église is only a small town, but contains several pleasant cafés, small hotels and a supermarket, and has a municipal camping site on its outskirts. Information is readily available from the *Office de Tourisme* (Tourist Information Office), close to the main square. The *Office de Tourisme* website is very useful, including details of local activities such as horse-riding, coarse fishing, bicycling, and rambling. One unusual place of interest is the *Cotentin Farm Museum* on the western side of the town, converted from an old working farm.

Close to Utah Beach itself is a campsite, *Utah-Beach Camping*, where caravans can be rented; the area also has activities such as archery, wind-surfing and sand yachting. There is a 9-hole golf course at Fontenay-sur-Mer. Montebourg to the north is larger, with more shops, and its own *Office de Tourisme*.

Carentan is a medium-sized town with all the standard amenities, and with its centre largely given over to shops and to car parking. The website of the *Office de Tourisme* offers information on local attractions and activities, including the large marina, the outdoor swimming pool, and facilities for canoeing and fishing, as well as tours of the marshes and the estuary area.

The area of the coast south of Utah Beach is designated as a wild bird sanctuary. The Cotentin and Bessin Marshland Park provides facilities for birdwatching from hides, and for exploring the marshes by boat or canoe, or on foot or bicycle, or even by horse or pack-saddled donkey. The park visitor centre is on the old N13 between Carentan and St-Côme-du-Mont.

THE UTAH BEACH TOURS

In addition to the general guidance on touring given above, the following points apply particularly to the Utah Beach tours. As already noted the IGN Série Bleue maps are the best for pinpointing locations exactly. The sheets needed for the Utah Beach battlefields are: *1310 Ouest* (St-Vaast-la-Hougue), *1311 Est* (Ste-Marie-du-Mont – Utah Beach), *1311 Ouest* (Ste-Mère-Église), *1312 Est* (Carentan), and *1312 Ouest* (Périers). The most commonly available road maps on sale locally are the Michelin 1:150,000 scale. *Map 303 Local: Calvados, Manche* covers the Normandy battlefield area. Roads and roads numbers change over the years, and it is important to use a map that is up to date.

These tours may be taken in any order, but suggestions for the best way to approach them are included below. Stands on the tours have been chosen to include locations with car-parks or with safe parking nearby in all cases. It is very important when parking to make sure that no obstruction is caused, and that there is no risk, especially to any children. This is a farming community, and large agricultural vehicles have every right to use the narrow country roads.

The main metalled road from Cherbourg through Montebourg and Ste-Mère-Église to Carentan and east to Isigny-sur-Mer, which was the Route Nationale N13, has been largely improved to be the motorway-class Autoroute A-13. At the time of writing and publication this improvement was continuing. Major directions on the A-13 are indicated by road signs as either CHERBOURG (northwards) or CAEN (eastwards). For some stretches the autoroute merges with the older N13; but at

Montebourg, Ste-Mère-Église and Carentan the A-13 by-passes the town while the old N13 still runs through the town, following the same route as in 1944. Junctions and directions on the A-13 and elsewhere are well signposted, particularly to locations associated with the Battle of Normandy, which are marked NORMANDIE 1944 – LE CHOC or OBJECTIF UN PORT.

American troops land on Utah Beach from a Landing Craft Tank (LCT) on D-Day. *(USNA)*

These tours are intended to give the visitor a feel for the battle and the terrain over which it was fought, going around the more important areas as well as stopping at specific sites. Many of the small villages on the tour routes are less than 5 km apart, and at driving speeds turnings are easy to miss, especially in the hedgerow country (travelling at 45 km/hr – just under 30 mph – means 750 metres a minute). For an example of the distances and times involved, some tourist brochures claim a driving time of 10–15 minutes from Ste-Mère-Église to Utah Beach. If taking any tour for the first time, then allow extra time, especially for wrong turnings; and if driving unaided then remember to watch the road as a first priority!

STARTING THE TOURS: For convenience, all tours are assumed to start on the A-13, either coming from Cherbourg or from Caen and Carentan.

BATTLEFIELD TOURS

BATTLEFIELD TOURS

TOUR A

THE MERDERET BRIDGEHEAD

OBJECTIVE: This tour looks at the principal sites fought for by the 82nd Airborne Division on D-Day and for the few days afterwards on either side of the River Merderet. This is a short tour of about half a day, but it fits well with Tour B. For the real enthusiast or expert on the battle, half a day could be spent walking around the sites at the Manoir de la Fière alone.

The commemorative stone in the memorial garden to 508th Parachute Infantry Regiment at Chef-du-Pont. *(Author)*

Stand A1: Les Forges Cemetery Marker

DIRECTIONS: Leave the A-13 at the junction with the D70 at les Forges, and follow signposts to Chef-du-Pont. Immediately after the D70 passes under the A-13, 50 metres on the left hand side there is a memorial marker. This identifies the former location, in the fields beyond, of one of three major American military cemeteries in the Ste-Mère-Église area, originally the burial site of 6,000 soldiers. In 1948 the dead from these cemeteries were either returned home or re-interred in the cemetery at Colleville-sur-Mer on Omaha Beach. There is a small parking place in front of the memorial. Stand facing north, with your back to the memorial.

THE ACTION: Les Forges crossroads with its small number of dwellings was one of the critical sites of the battle on D-Day. Its central position makes it a good place to take in the nature of the ground, and to get your bearings. Chef-du-Pont with its critical bridge is 3.5 km to the left along the D70, Ste-Marie-du-Mont is 5 km to the right along the same road, and Ste-Mère-Église is 3.5 km to the front up the N13. Landing Zone W for the American gliders stretched northwards from les Forges on either side of the N13. This location also marks the approximate furthest advance on D-Day by the main forces of 2/8th Infantry and 3/8th Infantry from Utah Beach, and by Howell Force later in the day. The pocket of ground still held by 795th Georgian Battalion on D-Day and D+1 is to the immediate right front, on the far side of the N13.

Stand A2: Chef-du-Pont Bridge

DIRECTIONS: Continue straight on the D70 for 3.5 km to Chef-du-Pont, turn left (still on the D70) under the railway bridge (this is a low bridge marked as 2.5 metres clearance, an alternative route via Pont l'Abbé is signposted). The bridge carries the railway line from Cherbourg, running roughly north to south. Continue straight on the D70 for 1 km to the bridge over the River Merderet. On the left is a milk factory, and immediately after that is a memorial garden to the battle with a car park. First, look round the memorial garden. A stone in the garden reads 'This Garden is Offered by 508th Airborne Veterans in Memory of June 1944 Fights – June 1978'. Directly opposite the garden on the far side of the D70 is another memorial stone to the 508th PIR. This is the centre of the fighting at Chef-du-Pont on D-Day. The road has been widened and a modern bridge has replaced the hump-backed stone bridge that existed in 1944. A sign gives the bridge's name as 'Pont du Capitain Roy Creek' in honour of the officer and men who defended the bridge against the last German counter-attack at 1700 hours on D-Day. Face northwards, with Chef-du-Pont village to your right and the bridge on your left. In 1944 the flooding of the river meant that

1 Captain Creek's force
2 Lt Col Ostberg's force
3 Lt Col Maloney's force
4 Lt Col Shanley's force
5 Lt Col Timmes' force
6 Airborne troops gathering at la Fière
7 1057th Grenadiers (elements)
8 1057th Grenadiers and
  100th Panzer T/R Battalion (elements)

a Cemetery markers

Base map: IGN 1311O

the meadows on either side of the road and bridge were swamps, and the road formed a causeway. The flooded area was overgrown with reeds, and in 1944 there were also more hedgerows and orchards. The Hill 30 position is about 1.5 km to your left front. Cauquigny and la Fière are just under 3 km directly ahead to the north. The main positions of 1057th Grenadiers were to your left, on the far side of the bridge.

The bridge over the River Merderet named after Captain Roy Creek at Chef-du-Pont, with a display panel showing the original bridge in 1944. *(Author)*

THE ACTION: Look to your right along the road from the bridge towards Chef-du-Pont. At 0900 hours on D-Day Brig Gen Gavin, assistant commander 82nd Airborne Division, ordered Lt Col Arthur Maloney with 75 men to leave la Fière for Chef-du-Pont. Shortly afterwards, receiving an incorrect report that Chef-du-Pont bridge was unguarded, Gavin took another 75 men under Lt Col Edwin J. Ostberg and headed for Chef-du-Pont, moving down the Cherbourg railway line. These were chiefly men of 507th PIR. Ostberg's troops reached Chef-du-Pont first.

> Men of Lt Col Ostberg's force recall the start of the battle against men of 1057th Grenadiers at Chef-du-Pont at about 1000 hours on D-Day.
>
> 'He found the village held by a light German force which was quickly driven out, retiring via the causeway across the river. They had positions dug in along the causeway

and took up fire posts there as they fell back. This was done in self-protection. The causeway was wholly exposed, and had they continued they would have had to run for 250 yards or more along an exposed defile... The Germans who had taken cover to the east of [the hump-backed] bridge could be shot from the positions where our men deployed along the river. The bridge, however, obstructed the view of the road beyond, and the enemy in the holes there were immune to small arms fire. The enemy appeared hesitant and reluctant to fight. One enemy soldier rose out of a foxhole attempting to surrender. A parachutist who was within a few feet of him, not seeing what the man intended, shot him in clear view of the others. Shortly afterwards, another German got up out of his foxhole in an attempt to surrender. He too was killed... No more of the enemy made any attempt to surrender, and the Americans had to fight for it throughout the day.'

Source: Combat Interviews, 82nd Airborne Division, US National Archives.

In the final German attack from the left attempting to cross the bridge at 1700, Captain Creek lost 14 out of his 34 men to German shellfire. His position was relieved next day by men of 508th PIR.

Stand A3: Hill 30

DIRECTIONS: Go straight on over the bridge and immediately turn right onto a minor road towards Gueutteville (note signpost). This is a narrow farm road with culverts on either side, and large vehicles may have difficulty. This road runs parallel with the River Merderet which is about 500 metres on the right hand side. The Hill 30 area, defended by Lt Col Shanley's force, is immediately on the left. This is not really visible as a 'hill', and in 1944 it had many more orchard trees. After 700 metres there is a T-junction at the hamlet of le-Port-Filiolet. Turn right towards Caponnet and Gueutteville, and after 500 metres turn right again towards Caponnet and Gueutteville. On the right hand side is Durécu Farm, with a blue plaque commemorating the battle displayed on the farm wall. Pull over to look round

The plaque marking the location of Hill 30 on the wall at Durécu Farm. The hill is directly opposite the farm on the far side of the road. *(Author)*

only if it is safe to do so, and if traffic will not be obstructed. Stand with your back to the plaque, facing west. This is close to the middle of the 82nd Airborne Division's drop area on D-Day. Hill 30 is in front, Drop Zone N is about 2.5 km to your right front, the River Merderet is directly behind you.

THE ACTION: Hill 30 was the area defended by the assembled force of 508th PIR under Lt Col Shanley from D-Day onwards. By holding this position in the centre, the paratroopers prevented the 1057th Grenadiers mounting an effective attack on either Chef-du-Pont bridge to the south or la Fière bridge to the north.

The Merderet at Chef-du-Pont, looking north-west. The area of Hill 30 is to the right. In 1944 the meadows on either side of the river were under water. *(Author)*

Private Frank Staples, D Company, 2/508th PIR, describes his experiences on Hill 30.

'I was the only one on Hill 30 with a Bazooka. I was not all that eager to get it. Joe Lutz was supposed to be my loader when he jumped in Normandy. He came out of the plane right behind me. I did not see him again for three

BATTLEFIELD TOURS

days. I never found the Bazooka they dropped either. They were dropped in equipment packs that were slung beneath the plane and dropped right after we were. I do not remember where I got the Bazooka I had... We were supposed to be there for three days. That's all the rations we carried. Before we got relieved, we were taking the cartridges out of our clips and loading them in the machine gun belts. They tried dropping us supplies, but most of it landed someplace else.'

Source: Dominique François, *The 508th Parachute Infantry Regiment*, p. 35.

Stand A4: The Manoir de la Fière

DIRECTIONS: Go straight on for 2 km through the hamlet of Caponnet to the village of Gueutteville. In the village centre take the right hand fork (no signpost) and then turn right onto the D15 (no signpost) towards Cauquigny and la Fière. As you turn, the area on the left is the eastern edge of Drop Zone N for 82nd Airborne Division, with Drop Zone T to the north. Go straight on for 1.5 km to the T-junction at Cauquigny, take the right hand fork (still the D15) for 650 metres over the bridge across the River Merderet at la Fière. The farmhouse of la Fière is on right hand side, now converted into *Le Café la Fière*. On the left is a memorial area for the battle with a car park.

First, walk around the area. The memorial has a prominent statue to the paratroopers on D-Day, named as 'Iron Mike' and inscribed: 'A Grateful Tribute to American Airborne Soldiers of D-Day – 6 June 1944 – 7 June 1997'. Nearby is an orientation table for the la Fière bridgehead battle in the stylised form of a collapsed parachute in metal and stone, and plaques to the airborne units that fought at la Fière. Walk uphill along the D15 about 200 metres towards Ste-Mère-Église. On the right hand side is a roped-off hole in the earth embankment beside the road. The plaque reads in French 'Here Fought General James M. Gavin on 6 June 1944', and the spot is traditionally regarded as Gavin's personal foxhole on D-Day, although this cannot be proved and is often taken with scepticism. Gavin's own after-action report described his command post as being at 'the railroad overpass' at la Fière, and the rail bridge is some distance

BATTLEFIELD TOURS

further on. Return to the orientation table next to the 'Iron Mike' statue and stand looking west across the Merderet. Cauquigny hamlet and church are 650 metres directly ahead across the water meadow, which was flooded in 1944. Amfréville is 2 km to your right front. Ste-Mère-Église is 3.5 km directly behind you.

The Manoir de la Fière, seen from the higher ground immediately to the north. The bridge over the River Merderet is visible on the right. The statue 'Iron Mike' and the memorial to the paratroopers are in the foreground. *(Author)*

THE ACTION: The American paratroopers assembled at la Fière on D-Day from several directions, but mainly from the north and north-west (the right as you are standing) on the far side of the Merderet. The first to reach la Fière on D-Day were A Company of 1/505th PIR, which had an almost uniquely good parachute landing to the east of the railway line (directly behind your position) and had assembled all its men except two within an hour of the drop. The company spent the rest of D-Day heavily involved in the fighting at la Fière, losing 12 men killed and 40 wounded (including attached troops from other units).

> **Brig Gen James M. Gavin describes the attack by troops of 1057th Grenadiers and 100th T/R Panzer Battalion across the la Fière causeway on D-Day.**
>
> 'I then went back to la Fière bridge, arriving there in the latter part of the afternoon. The fighting had greatly increased in intensity. German mortar and high velocity

The view from the 'nose' of higher ground at la Fière mentioned in Brig Gen Gavin's account, on which the 'Iron Mike' statue now stands, looking west across the River Merderet (in the foreground) towards Cauquigny hamlet and church in the distance. In 1944 the intervening flood plain was under water. *(Author)*

artillery fire was coming down on the nose [of high ground] overlooking the bridge... The situation rapidly developed to a very serious stage. I sent an officer courier to Lt Col [Arthur] Maloney [507th PIR, at Chef-du-Pont] instructing him to bring all his force, less a platoon, with a couple of automatic weapons which I figured would be enough to hold his position on the Chef-du-Pont causeway... The German reaction continued to build in intensity. They were evidently making a strong effort to cross the bridge [at la Fière], and at about 8 p.m. managed to get a foothold in our position on the east bank. Our position on the nose overlooking the bridge was, in the opinion of the battalion commander, becoming untenable, partly due to the intense high velocity artillery fire and small arms fire directed against our exposed positions on the forward slopes overlooking the bridge. Lt Col Maloney was directed to deploy his force on both sides of the main road leading to the causeway, to attack through the [505th PIR], re-establish our position overlooking the bridge, to contact Major [Frederick] Kellam [commanding 1/505th PIR] and for them both to hold that position until orders were received.'

Source: Combat Interviews, 82nd Airborne Division, US National Archives.

Your viewing point is on the 'nose' of ground described in Brig Gen Gavin's report. Retrace your route back over the bridge and along the road towards Cauquigny church and hamlet (the distance is about 650 metres and some may prefer not to walk). In 1944 this road was a causeway with inundations on either side. On the right hand side is a marker post reading in French 'Flooding on 6 June 1944 to the 7th Mark', showing the height of the water. Go straight on to Cauquigny church. Stand facing northwards towards Drop Zone T.

The view from Cauquigny eastward across the River Merderet flood plain towards the 'nose' of higher ground mentioned in Brig Gen Gavin's account. The white marble base of the 'Iron Mike' statue is just visible as a point of light on the high ground. (Author)

Lt Col Charles J. Timmes, commanding 2/507th PIR, describes his landing in the River Merderet inundations near the Cauquigny–la Fière causeway in darkness at about 0230 hours on D-Day.

'Timmes landed on the west side of the Merderet river about 1,000 yards east of Amfréville. That put him in a swamp and in water up to his knees. There was quite a bit of wind and he couldn't stop the chute. As he moved along with the chute pulling him, the water sometimes gave off to depths of four feet or so, and then shelved up again. He was able to check his motion and free himself when he got to an embankment along a drainage ditch. In this kind of experience where the chute is pulling a man along through water and over uneven ground, a large part of the time the man is being pulled along flat, and with his head under water, so that he is fighting always to recover his balance at the same time that he is trying to stop the chute. Timmes says that he at times felt that he was in danger of drowning, and that this was a common experience of the men who came down in the swamp area. The waterlogging of the equipment added to the difficulties of getting out of the harness and of getting to a knife so as to cut loose. Timmes estimates that it was probably 20 minutes before he could free himself.'

Source: Combat Interviews, 82nd Airborne Division, US National Archives.

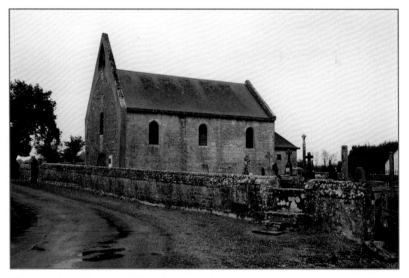

The church and hamlet of Cauquigny, on the far side of the causeway road from la Fière. *(Author)*

From this position at Cauquigny church look back to the right towards the 'Iron Mike' statue. This is the perspective of the attacking Germans of 1057th Grenadiers and 100th Panzer T/R Battalion on D-Day, and shows the critical importance of the 'nose' of high ground.

Resume the tour by leaving the la Fière car park, turn left onto the D15 for 3 km towards Ste-Mère-Église. Just before entering the town turn right at a crossroads to Vaulaville and straight on through the village to the T-junction with the D67 from Chef-du-Pont. Turn left onto the D67 towards Ste-Mère-Église. After 300 metres, just before entering the town, on the right hand side there is another cemetery marker, recording the burial of 5,000 American soldiers. There is a small parking area next to the memorial if you wish to stop.

TO CONCLUDE THE TOUR: Drive into Ste-Mère-Église and follow signs to the A-13.

TO CONTINUE WITH TOUR B: Enter the town and park in or close to the main square.

TOUR B

SAINTE-MÈRE-ÉGLISE

OBJECTIVE: This tour looks at Ste-Mère-Église, and at some of the principal actions fought by 82nd Airborne and 101st Airborne to the east of the N13 on D-Day that were not directly connected with the Utah Beach landings. When combined with Tour A it provides an all-round look at the airborne achievement on D-Day.

Stand B1: Sainte-Mère-Église

DIRECTIONS: The town is well signposted from the A-13. Park in or close to the main square. Start in the square facing the church. Ste-Mère-Église itself is a major tourist centre that is often used as a base by visitors looking at the battlefields, and has several souvenir shops and cafés as well as an outstanding museum. It is quite possible to spend all day (or longer) seeing all the sights associated with the battle here.

THE ACTION: The main square with its church has become what is in effect one large memorial to the D-Day battle and the role of the American airborne forces. There are several plaques and boards around the square dedicated to notable people or pointing out that a nearby house was the scene of a famous event. One monument stone is to Alexandre Renaud (1891–1966), in tribute both to his work as mayor on D-Day and as a historian who documented many of the events of the battle as they affected the town.

Mayor Alexandre Renaud describes the parachute landings at Ste-Mère-Église in the early hours of D-Day.

'Sainte-Mère-Église was in trouble, and the church was calling for help [by the sound of its bells ringing]. Just at that moment, a big transport plane, all lights ablaze, flew right over the tree-tops, followed immediately by others, and yet others. They came from the west in great waves, almost silent, their giant shadows covering the earth. Suddenly, what looked like huge confetti dropped out of their fuselages and fell quickly to earth. Paratroopers! The work at the pump stopped, all eyes were raised, and the Flak started firing. All around us, paratroopers were landing with a heavy thud on the ground. By the light of the fire, we saw a man manipulating the cables of his parachute. Another, less skilful, came down in the middle of the flames. Sparks flew, and the fire burned brighter. The legs of the paratrooper contracted violently as they were hit. His raised arms came down. The giant parachute, billowing in the wind, rolled over the field with the inert body.'

Source: Alexandre Renaud, *Sainte-Mère-Église*, pp. 36–7.

The church of Notre Dame de la Paix in the main square, Ste-Mère-Église. *(Author)*

The main square is dominated by the church of Notre Dame de la Paix. The church bells were rung on the night of D-Day as a fire alarm in response to the burning building on the south-east side of the square. Inside the church is a memorial window to the American paratroopers, and a Liberation memorial window donated by 82nd Airborne Division veterans, dated 6 June 1969. On the exterior of the church, fixed to the tower, is a stone figure of a parachutist, with a fabric parachute attached, snagged on part of the tower. This commemorates a D-Day episode made especially famous by Cornelius Ryan's best selling book *The Longest Day* and the feature film (1962) based on it.

Private John Steele of 505th PIR was one of the paratroopers who came down onto Ste-Mère-Église, being wounded in the foot by a bullet as he descended. Steele landed on the roof of the church and his parachute caught on the tower.

'Private Steele, his parachute draped over the steeple of the church, hung just under the eaves. He heard the shouts and the screams. He saw Germans and Americans firing at each other in the square and the streets. And, almost paralysed by terror, he saw winking red flashes of machine-guns as streams of stray bullets shot past and over him. Steele had tried to cut himself down. But his

knife had somehow slipped out of his hand and dropped to the square below. Steele then decided that his only hope lay in playing dead. On the roof, only a few yards away from him, German machine-gunners fired at everything in sight, but not at Steele.'

Source: Cornelius Ryan, *The Longest Day*, pp. 112–3.

The church tower and stone paratrooper. *(Jonathan Falconer)*

At least one other soldier of 505th PIR who jumped along with Steele, Private Ken Russell, had his parachute snag on the

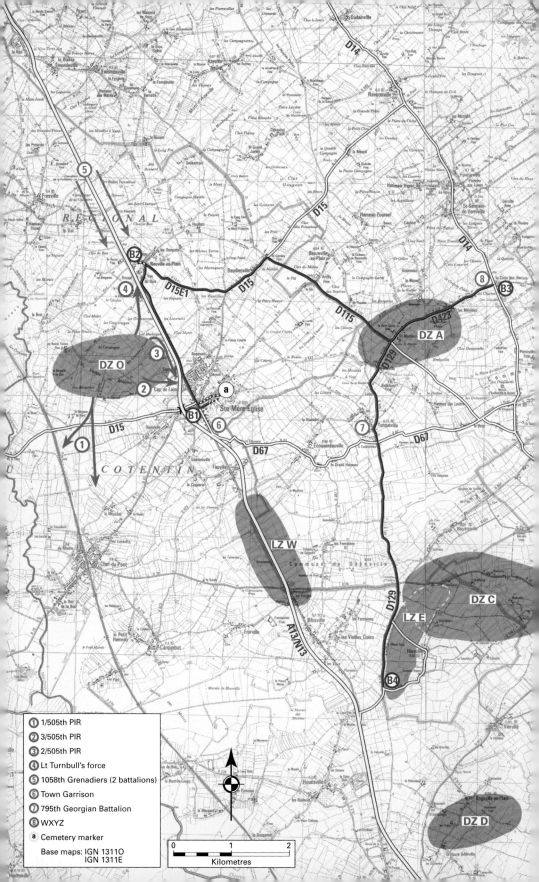

1 1/505th PIR

2 3/505th PIR

3 2/505th PIR

4 Lt Turnbull's force

5 1058th Grenadiers (2 battalions)

6 Town Garrison

7 795th Georgian Battalion

8 WXYZ

a Cemetery marker

Base maps: IGN 1311O
IGN 1311E

DZ O

DZ A

DZ C

DZ D

LZ W

LZ E

Ste-Mère-Église

0   1   2
Kilometres

Sainte-Mère-Église Airborne Museum

Musée Airborne Sainte-Mère-Eglise, 14 Rue Eisenhower, 50480 Sainte-Mère-Eglise; tel: +33 (0)2 33 41 41 35; web: <www.Airborne-museum.org>. Open daily 0900–1845 Apr–Sept, 0930–1200 and 1400–1800 Feb–Mar and Oct–Nov, closed Dec & Jan. Admission charge; nearby parking.

tower as well, but he cut himself free with his trench knife and dropped to the ground. Russell believed that the heat from the fire sucked the parachutes towards it as the men descended.

If the statue marking Private Steele's position on the church tower looks too conspicuous for him to have survived, it is because it is on the wrong side of the church, facing towards the open square for ease of viewing. Steele hung on the opposite side of the church for about two hours until spotted by two soldiers of 919th Grenadiers stationed in the belltower as lookouts, who brought him inside. Injured and shaken, Steele remained a prisoner for another two hours until the town was liberated.

Opposite the church on the far side of the square, built partly on the location of the burning house that led to the fire alarm on the night of D-Day, is the *Musée Airborne Sainte-Mère-Église*. The foundation stone for this museum was laid in 1961 by General Gavin. This museum has been for years a centre for American airborne veterans. In addition to other displays, two hangars in the shape of giant stylised parachutes house a CG-4A Waco glider, and a C-47 Dakota 4100825 *Argonia* of 92nd Troop Carrier Squadron that flew paratroopers of 82nd Airborne Division into battle on the night of D-Day.

Starting from the main square is a tourist circuit marked by prominent boards numbered 0–15 with the featured locations nearby. This circuit takes the tourist on foot away from the church and main square, and back again. It takes about an hour to walk and includes several sites of interest, not all of them directly related to D-Day, but (at present) the route between the locations is not well indicated and it requires some perseverance or a guide to find everything. Stand 0 is directly opposite the museum, followed by Stand 1, which is the town pump from which water was obtained to fight the fires on the night of D-Day. Stand 3, away from the main square to the north-east, is the third of the cemetery markers, recording the burial of 3,000 American soldiers. Some of the sites relate to the town's own losses on D-Day, which included 22 civilians killed.

BATTLEFIELD TOURS

Then: The main street in the centre of Ste-Mère-Église, on 8 June 1944. *(USNA)*

Now: The same view of the main street of Ste-Mère-Église, now renamed the Rue Général de Gaulle, looking south. The town square is to the left. *(Author)*

Stands 11–14 are all in or near the *hôtel de ville* (town hall), which is on the road uphill from the north side of the square. These stands include, outside the *hôtel de ville*, the 'Kilometre 0' marker stone (*see Tour D*) with a plaque stating that: 'This was the first town to be liberated on the western front 5–6 June 1944'. It was outside the *hôtel de ville* that Lt Col Krause of 3/505th PIR raised the US flag at 0430 hours on D-Day. Ste-Mère-Église's claim to be the first town liberated on D-Day therefore seems valid, although according to US Army combat interviews 'The flag was raised before dawn, Krause pulled it down a few minutes later because the pole was wobbly'.

The *hôtel de ville* at Ste-Mère-Église, with the 'Kilometre 0' marker prominent in the foreground. *(Author)*

Stand B2: Neuville-au-Plain

DIRECTIONS: Leave Ste-Mère-Église and take the main N13 road northwards towards Montebourg. On the left hand side of this stretch of the A-13 is Drop Zone O for the 82nd Airborne Division.

Lt Col Edward Krause of 3/505th PIR describes parachuting onto Drop Zone O southwest of Neuville-au-Plain on the night of D-Day.

'I would say that in the next three minutes I came as close to being crashed in the air as I ever hope to be. The pilot

called for evasive action and we split up. Some went high, some went lower, others right and left. This split our formation and we were well spread. Just about two or three minutes before the drop time, we saw the green T [signal lights], it was a Godsend and I felt that I had found the Holy Grail. I would say that I dropped from over 2000 feet. It was the longest ride I have ever had in over fifty jumps, and while descending, four ships [aircraft] passed under me and I really sweated that out.'

Source: Official record of an Operation Neptune debriefing conference, 13 August 1944.

Leave the N13 after 1.5 km at the next junction and follow signs northwards for a further 500 metres to Neuville-au-Plain. Enter the village and park close to the church on the right hand side. Walk the short distance along the main road through the village, past the château, to within sight of the N13/A-13. Stand facing northwards with the château on your right. Ste-Mère-Église is directly behind you, Drop Zone O is the area on the far side of the main road to your left rear. The River Merderet and the Cherbourg railway line are 2.5 km to your left, parallel to the main road. The main German counterattack from the north on D-Day, by 1058th Grenadiers, came directly down the main road to your front from Montebourg 7 km away.

THE ACTION: Just north of your position and on either side of the main road was the scene of 1058th Infantry's first attempts on 6–7 June to break through the American defences to the north of Ste-Mère-Église. The defence on D-Day in the hedgerows north and on either side of Neuville-au-Plain was led by Lieutenant Turner 'Chief' Turnbull of 3rd Platoon, D Company, 2/505th PIR, who was half-Cherokee Native American.

Men of 3rd Platoon, D Company, 2/505th PIR, describe the start of their ambush of the advance by 1058th Grenadiers at Neuville-au-Plain at 1030 hours on D-Day.

'There were 42 men in the platoon... They then proceeded about 40 yards beyond the hamlet and set up a road block north of the houses, and covering it with a bazooka and two riflemen. To the right of the [Cherbourg] road was convenient high ground and the machinegun and most of

The village church at Neuville-au-Plain, to the north of Ste-Mère-Église.
Battle damage from 1944 is clearly visible on the church tower. *(Author)*

the platoon were disposed on that side. However, one squad was to the left of the road... They were in this position only about 30 minutes and then the Germans moved against them from the north. About one company of Germans were seen coming down the road by the men on the right, although they were not visible to the squad on the left flank. They were marching in column of twos, and were not delivering any fire forward... The two right-hand squads at the rear had begun to fire on the enemy and the Germans had deployed along the hedges and ditches. They were replying to this fire from the front and had not yet detected the position of the men on the left.'

Source: Combat Interviews, 82nd Airborne Division, US National Archives.

This was the start of a protracted firefight that lasted most of the day. Turnbull was killed by artillery fire on 7 June. This small action, by holding up the northern arm of the German pincer attack on Ste-Mère-Église, enabled the Americans to defeat the attack of the southern arm and to secure the town.

Stand B3: Objective WXYZ

DIRECTIONS: Retrace your route and leave Neuville-au-Plain going southwards, taking the left hand fork from the church onto the D15E1. After 1.5 km turn left at the T-junction onto the D15 through Baudienville. This road and the surrounding area represent the northern edge of the American lodgement at the end of D-Day. The route follows approximately the area of no-man's-land between the 82nd Airborne Division at Ste-Mère-Église and the 101st Airborne Division to the east.

After Baudienville, at the crossroads with the D115 turn right. Carry straight on along the D115 for just over 2.5 km (the road numbering southwards along the D115 is potentially confusing: carry straight on at the crossroads with the D17 and again past the left hand turn onto the D129). At the crossroads with the D423, turn left towards St-Martin-de-Vareville (note that the right hand turn towards Turqueville and Ste-Mère-Église is also numbered as the D129). Go straight on along the D423 for just under 3 km. The area on either side of the road just before les Mézières (given as Mésières on some American maps) is Drop Zone A for the 101st Airborne on D-Day. Go through les Mézières and straight on over the crossroads with the D14 coastal ridge road. Park safely and walk back to the D423/D14 crossroads. Stand facing west, back along the D423 towards les Mézières. The D14 coastal ridge road, like the N13, was a critical north–south communications artery for the Germans. Directly behind you is St-Martin-de-Varreville and Exits 3 and 4 from Utah Beach. The 122-mm battery position of 1/1261st Coastal Artillery was in the fields to your left rear. The farm buildings on the right hand side along the D14 are on (or close to) the building Objective W, commandeered by 1/502nd PIR as a command post on D-Day. The remaining buildings of Objective XYZ were on either side of the D423 towards les Mézières. Walk along the road towards les Mézières following the action on the map.

THE ACTION: The main focus on D-Day for Lt Col Cassidy commanding 1/502nd PIR was to secure Exits 3 and 4 from Utah Beach, but the WXYZ position was the scene of one of the most remarkable episodes of D-Day. At about 0600 hours, Cassidy ordered Staff Sergeant Harrison Summers to take 15 men, few of them from 1/502nd PIR and most of them unknown to Summers,

BATTLEFIELD TOURS

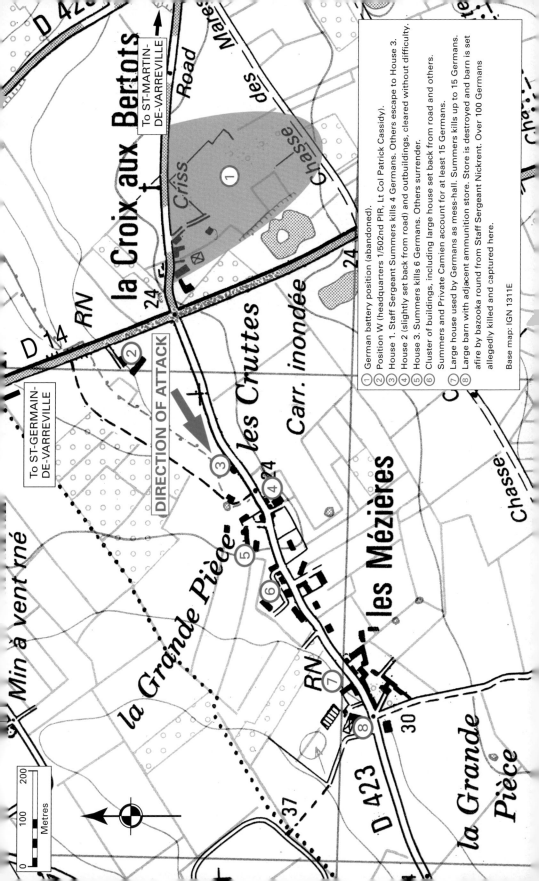

la Croix aux Bertots

To ST-MARTIN-DE-VARREVILLE

D 428

Criss

Road

Chasse des Marais

RN

24

24

D 14

RN

To ST-GERMAIN-DE-VARREVILLE

DIRECTION OF ATTACK

les Cruttes

Carr. inondée

Chasse

les Mézières

la Grande Pièce

Min à vent rné

RN

30

D 423

37

la Grande Pièce

Metres

0 100 200

① German battery position (abandoned).

② Position W (headquarters 1/502nd PIR, Lt Col Patrick Cassidy).

③ House 1. Staff Sergeant Summers kills 4 Germans. Others escape to House 3.

④ House 2 (slightly set back from road) and outbuildings, cleared without difficulty.

⑤ House 3. Summers kills 6 Germans. Others surrender.

⑥ Cluster of buildings, including large house set back from road and others. Summers and Private Camien account for at least 15 Germans.

⑦ Large house used by Germans as mess-hall. Summers kills up to 15 Germans.

⑧ Large barn with adjacent ammunition store. Store is destroyed and barn is set afire by bazooka round from Staff Sergeant Nickrent. Over 100 Germans allegedly killed and captured here.

Base map: IGN 1311E

to clear the XYZ buildings. The houses and buildings that made up the barracks complex all had thick stone walls with fire slots in them. Summers' first objective was three houses, two on the right of the road and one on the left.

The crossroads of the D14 coastal ridge road with the D423 near les Mezières, the start of the location in 1944 of the WXYZ buildings. *(Author)*

Report by Colonel S.L.A. Marshall, US Army official historian, on the start of Staff Sergeant Harrison Summers' actions at XYZ on D-Day.

'He walked right up to the first house and kicked the door in. The Germans inside were firing through the slots and he burst in on them before they could turn. He shot four of them with a Tommy gun [Thompson sub-machinegun]. Others, including some French civilians, had run out of the rear and escaped to building Number 3. The Number 2 house [on the left of the road] was taken without difficulty, then a [30-calibre] machinegun manned by Private William A. Burt was set up on the road at 50 yards distance to fire on the Number 3 house. The Germans replied with rifles and machine pistols but the machinegun fire, aimed at the embrasures, made them keep their heads down and fire wildly. [Lieutenant Elmer] Brandenberger and Summers ran for the door and just as they came up to the wall, something exploded next to

Brandenberger, knocking him down and mangling his left arm. Summers went on by himself and smashed the door in, firing as he did it. There were six Germans inside: he Tommy-gunned them before they could move.'

Source: '101st Airborne Division During Neptune', US National Archives.

At some point relatively early in the action Summers was joined by a captain of the 82nd Airborne Division whom he did not recognise, and who was killed by a German sniper before he could render useful assistance. However, his death prompted Private John Camien to move forward to help Summers in what up to now had been an almost single-handed fight. Pausing to recover their breath before each charge, the two men cleared several buildings, killing at least 15 more Germans. They worked swapping weapons, one attacking with Summers' Thompson while the other gave covering fire with Camien's carbine, with Private Burt on the light machine gun providing support. Two buildings were left. Summers charged one and kicked the door down. Inside, some 15 Germans were seated round a table having breakfast. Summers reportedly shot them all.

One of the modern farm buildings on the northern side of the D423 close to what was the WXYZ position in 1944. *(Author)*

The last building was a large long barn-like structure, with 70 metres of open field to cross to reach it. Several of the soldiers following up with Summers were hit by a German sniper. They tried to rush across this gap; four more were killed and four were wounded and the rest took cover again. Private Burt fired tracer at a haystack and ammunition store beside it, setting them on fire and causing the ammunition to explode. Thirty Germans ran out of the shed and were shot down.

At this point Staff Sergeant Roy Nickrent arrived from Cassidy's command post with a bazooka. He fired seven rounds into the building's roof, setting it on fire. Someone also fired 60-mm mortar shells at the building, but these appear to have missed. As the building burned, over 80 Germans tried to escape from it. At least 50 were cut down by the Americans; 31 made it to the hedges where they surrendered. It was 1530 hours and Summers, who had been fighting for at least five hours, relaxed and lit a cigarette. He had killed or captured over 150 Germans, at times almost single-handedly. When asked how he felt he replied, 'Not very good, it was all kind of crazy.' Summers was awarded the Distinguished Service Cross for his achievement.

Stand B4: The Brigadier General Pratt Memorial

DIRECTIONS: From the D423/D14 WXYZ crossroads retrace your route on the D423 back through Les Mézières, going straight on at the crossroads with the D115 towards Turqueville. The road for this stretch is the D129; ignore any junctions with minor roads or tracks. This is the area of the furthest advance westward by 1/8th Infantry on D-Day, facing 795th Georgian Battalion. Go straight on through Turqueville (the road is still the D129) and straight on for a further 4 km past the D129 crossroads with the D70. About 600 metres before the D129 reaches the A-13, it forms a T-junction with the D329 from Hiesville. At this T-junction on the left hand side is the memorial to Brig Gen Donald F. Pratt, assistant divisional commander of the 101st Airborne, who died when his glider landed in this field at about 0355 hours on D-Day. Stand facing this memorial. The area to your right front is Landing Zone E for the 101st Airborne, the westward extension of Drop Zone C. The memorial stone places the actual site of the glider crash 280 metres to the east.

The wreckage of a CG-4A Waco glider that landed too close to the trees and hedgerows near Utah Beach, including a destroyed jeep and one American fatality. Photograph taken on 7 June. *(USNA)*

THE ACTION: There are many stories, and even some legends, surrounding Brig Gen Pratt's death, which came from a broken neck. He was flown in the lead glider of the first wave of the Chicago Mission by Lt Col 'Mike' Murphy of 434th Troop Carrier Group, regarded as the finest glider pilot in the US Army, with 2nd Lieutenant John M. Butler as co-pilot. It is generally accepted that the glider was overweight (perhaps from additional armour plating protecting Pratt's jeep) and that his head struck a cross-beam with the impact of landing because he was sitting up high in his jeep in the cargo area. The casualty rate from the glider landings on D-Day shows that these landings carried a risk regardless of rank. Murphy's co-pilot was killed outright in the landing, while Pratt's aide de camp, sitting behind him in his jeep, escaped unharmed. Although LZ E was marked with lights, one of the gliders smashed into them on landing, forcing the rest to land by moonlight.

Murphy's usual glider was the *Fighting Falcon*, with its name painted on its nose. On 3 June he requested a Griswold Nose (a reinforced nose section) for his glider. Since there was no time to make the alteration, Murphy was given a new glider onto which was painted the same inscription as on the original: 'Fighting Falcon presented by Greenville Schools, Greenville, Michigan'. This glider also had a number 1 painted on its nose for the flight and landing, while the original *Fighting Falcon*, flown by 1st Lieutenant Robert Butler, became number 45.

A crashed CG-4A Waco glider on D-Day. *(USNA)*

1st Lieutenant Victor B. Warriner, flying glider number 2 on the Chicago Mission, watches the landing of the *Fighting Falcon* on Landing Zone E on D-Day.

'Warriner landed first and as his crew was getting out of the glider a dull thud set the ground shaking. Murphy had just landed. He had come in too fast and when he tried to brake his Waco skidded on the wet grass and ended up crashing into a tree in the middle of a hedge. Murphy was held in his seat harness amid a tangle of tubes and fabric. Coming to, he managed to pull himself clear of the wreckage, but with both legs broken. He saw that his co-pilot had been killed instantly, his disjointed body lying in what was left of the front airframe... Murphy turned down an offer of morphine so as to have a clear head to defend himself, and asked for someone to go and see how

Brigadier General Pratt was doing. [Captain] Van Gorder climbed into the Waco and found him in the passenger seat of the jeep with his helmet still on. The crash landing had broken his neck. He was the highest ranking [American] officer killed on D-Day.'

Source: Philippe Esvelin, *D-Day Gliders*, p. 85.

TO CONCLUDE THE TOUR: Return to the D129 and continue straight on to the A-13.

TO CONTINUE WITH TOUR A: Retrace the route to the crossroads with the D70, turn left towards les Forges and Chef-du-Pont.

TO CONTINUE WITH TOUR D: Take the A-13 to Ste-Mère-Église (perhaps for a mid-day break).

TO CONTINUE WITH TOUR E: Continue straight on along the D129 to the A-13 and come off at St-Côme-du-Mont.

TOUR C

THE ATLANTIC WALL

OBJECTIVE: This tour looks at the German Atlantic Wall defences to the north of Utah Beach. The tour is intended for those particularly interested in fortifications, who might easily spend half a day on the Atlantic Wall and northern flank defences at Quinéville, Crisbecq and Azeville. Others might prefer to take these more quickly and include another tour in the same day or even half-day.

Stand C1: The Quinéville Blockhouse

DIRECTIONS: Leave the A-13 and take the N13 into Montebourg, and then the D42 northeast to Quinéville. This road was the German main line of resistance on 12–13 June 1944. Follow the D42 for 4.5 km to the crossroads with the D14, the coastal ridge road, noting the sign for the *Musée de la Liberté* in Quinéville. Continue straight on for 2 km through Quinéville towards the coast and Quinéville harbour (given as 'le Havre' on some maps). Just beyond Quinéville is a bridge over a culvert with a German blockhouse on the left hand side, part of a resistance nest. Park where it is safe and walk back to the blockhouse. Stand facing southward, away from the blockhouse.

The German blockhouse just east of Quinéville, a typical example of the Atlantic Wall defences. *(Author)*

THE ACTION: The view in front of you is a good example of the hedgerow country. The German front line on 12 June began 2–3 km away across the fields directly to your front, with positions in depth all the way back to the D42 and beyond to the north. The front line at Fontenay-sur-Mer and Dangueville was about 3.5 km to your right front. The strongpoint 'Ginster Hill', including the headquarters and a naval battery of 1261st Army Coastal Artillery Regiment, was on the high ground to the northwest, about 1.5 km behind you to your right.

> *Oberstleutnant* (Lt-Col) Günther Keil, commanding Battlegroup *Keil* (originally commanding 919th Grenadier Regiment), describes the situation on 12 June 1944.
>
> 'My right [westerly] wing was hanging loose, jutting out almost a thousand metres. Only a thin security line established the connection to the 2nd Battalion of the

920th Regiment of Battlegroup Rohrbach lying farther to the rear, and protected my open right flank. On the morning of 12 June General Marcks [commanding LXXXIV Corps] appeared and, having explained the situation, ordered that the Marcouf [Crisbecq] Battery be given up and the front be withdrawn to the southern edge of the village of Fontenay-sur-Mer [as far as the] south-western edge of Dangueville. The line Montebourg–Quinéville had already been ordered as the main line of resistance that had to be held by all means; as far as possible, the enemy had to be stopped south of this line.'

Source: Adapted from David C. Isby, *Fighting in Normandy*, p. 145.

It was after making this tour of his forces that General Marcks was killed later in the day. The order to evacuate the Crisbecq battery was given late on 11 June and General Marcks presumably confirmed this decision early next day, or ordered that no attempt should be made to recapture it.

Stand C2: Quinéville Musée de la Liberté

DIRECTIONS: Go straight on along the D42 to the coast. Just before the seafront is the *Musée de la Liberté*. Built in part over a German blockhouse, this museum is dedicated to reflecting life in the region under the German occupation from 1940 onwards and the impact of liberation on the civilian population in 1944.

Quinéville Museum of Liberty

Musée de la Liberté, Avenue de la Plage, 50310 Quinéville; tel: +33 (0)2 33 21 40 44. Open daily 0930–1930 June–Sept, otherwise 1000–1800; closed mid-Nov to mid-March. Admission charge; free parking.

THE ACTION: Quinéville was the northernmost of the planned objectives for D-Day if all went perfectly for the Americans. Outside the museum is a display stating that, on the night of 26–27 December 1943, Lieutenant Francis Vourch and a team of five Frenchmen from the British Army's 10th (Inter-Allied) Commando came ashore at Quinéville to reconnoitre the area as part of the Allied preparations for D-Day. There is also a marker stone for the *Voie de la Liberté* (Road to Liberty – *see* the Utah

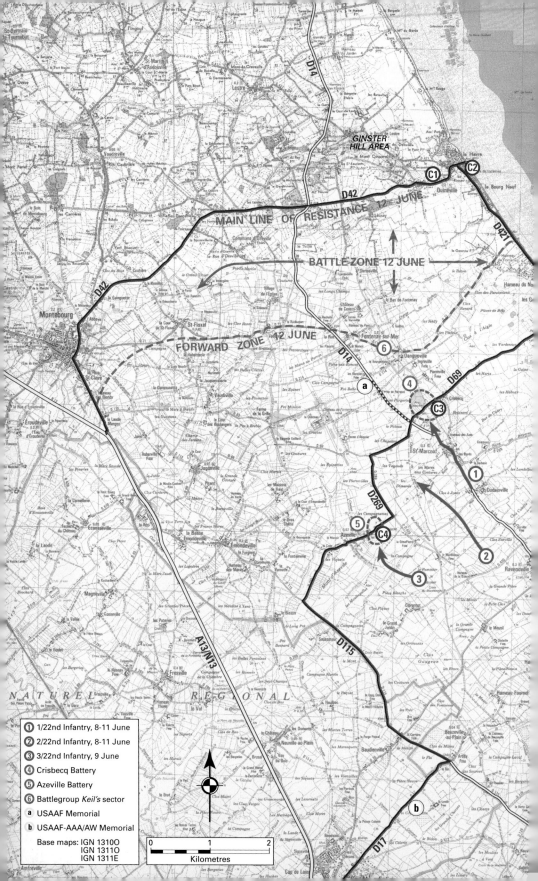

GINSTER
HILL AREA

C1   C2

D14

D42

MAIN LINE OF RESISTANCE 12 JUNE

D421

BATTLE ZONE 12 JUNE

D42

Montebourg

St-Floxel

FORWARD ZONE 12 JUNE

6   Fontenay-sur-Mer

D14

Dangueville

D69

a   4   C3

St-Marcouf

1   Dodainville

Éroudeville

Émondeville

D269

5   C4

2   Ravenoville

Azeville

3

A13/N13

D115

N A T U R E L   R E G I O N A L

D17   b

1	1/22nd Infantry, 8–11 June
2	2/22nd Infantry, 8–11 June
3	3/22nd Infantry, 9 June
4	Crisbecq Battery
5	Azeville Battery
6	Battlegroup *Keil's* sector
a	USAAF Memorial
b	USAAF-AAA/AW Memorial

Base maps: IGN 1310O
IGN 1311O
IGN 1311E

0   1   2
Kilometres

Beach stand in Tour D for an explanation). Walk down to the beach, where resistance nest positions are still intact. The Îles St-Marcouf, the first soil of France liberated from the sea on D-Day, are visible out to sea. This is a good location from which to get an appreciation of the German view of the landings and fighting.

Stand C3: The Crisbecq Battery

DIRECTIONS: Leave the museum taking the D42 back towards Quinéville, but immediately turn left onto the D421, the coastal road. Go straight on south for 3 km through les Gougins. Note the Atlantic Wall blockhouses, remains of resistance nests, on both sides of the road. At the T-junction immediately after les Gougins turn right onto the D69 towards Crisbecq and St-Marcouf, and straight on for about 2.5 km through Crisbecq village. The Crisbecq battery is well signposted 400 metres past the village, with blockhouses or casemates on both sides of the road and a car park on the left hand side. Walk around the site, and then stand at the observation platform on top of the command bunker next to the car park, looking out to sea. The Îles St-Marcouf should be visible in good weather, together with the entire deployment area for Task Force U on D-Day. Utah Beach is about 11 km to your right front. The American advance to capture the battery came from the south, directly to your right.

View from the observation platform at the Crisbecq battery, looking east towards the beach across the water meadows that were flooded in 1944. *(Author)*

THE ACTION: The Crisbecq battery, also known as the Marcouf battery or the Marcouf naval battery, was attached to 1261st Army Coastal Artillery Regiment, but crewed by a garrison of 300 middle aged naval reservists under *Oberleutnant-zur-See* (Lieutenant) Walter Ohmsen. It was first attacked by Allied bombers on 19 April, and attacks together with construction demands from other locations slowed the battery's construction. On 6 June 1944 it had four 210-mm Skoda guns, but casemates completed for only two of them, with the others and a single 150-mm gun still in the open, plus six 75-mm and three 20-mm anti-aircraft guns, protected by 17 machine-guns. A minefield 300 metres deep protected the position, with a triple line of barbed wire. *Generalmajor* Gerhard Triepel, in charge of coastal artillery in the Cotentin, remembered the battery as also having a 40-mm gun on a wheeled carriage 2 km to the north at the Château de Courcy, near Fontenay-sur-Mer.

The observation post, command bunker and fire control position for the Crisbecq battery. A modern viewing platform and orientation table have been built on top of the structure. *(Author)*

This battery was well known as the most powerful in the area. On 7 June, the OKW War Diary, amid its record of the grand scale of the landings, noted that, 'The Marcouf heavy naval coastal battery, which periodically had been inactive, could again partake in the battle', although shelling by Allied cruisers repeatedly silenced it again.

The view along the gun barrel of the 210-mm gun in its casemate at the Crisbecq battery, looking out to sea. *(USNA)*

Next to the car park is the command bunker, which also acted as the fire control bunker for the Azeville Battery. The two gun casemates are in the field on the far side of the road. There is a small one-room display with information about the battery inside the command bunker; the entrance is from the road through a hedge rather than from the car park, and not obvious. (This also makes the battery a good picnic site with a place to shelter if it is raining). The roofs of the casemates were collapsed and the guns removed by US Engineers as part of demolition after its capture.

Stand C4: The Azeville Battery

DIRECTIONS: Leave the Crisbecq battery and carry straight on westwards to the crossroads with the D14 (the coastal ridge road). As an option to view a small USAAF memorial, turn right towards Fontenay-sur-Mer (note that 'sur-mer' – 'on sea' is misleading for this inland village), then go straight on for about 800 metres just past la Perette farm on the left. Between this farm and the next crossroads with the D214 is a marker stone about a metre high on the left hand side (it can be hard to spot if the crops in the field behind it are well grown). This memorial was

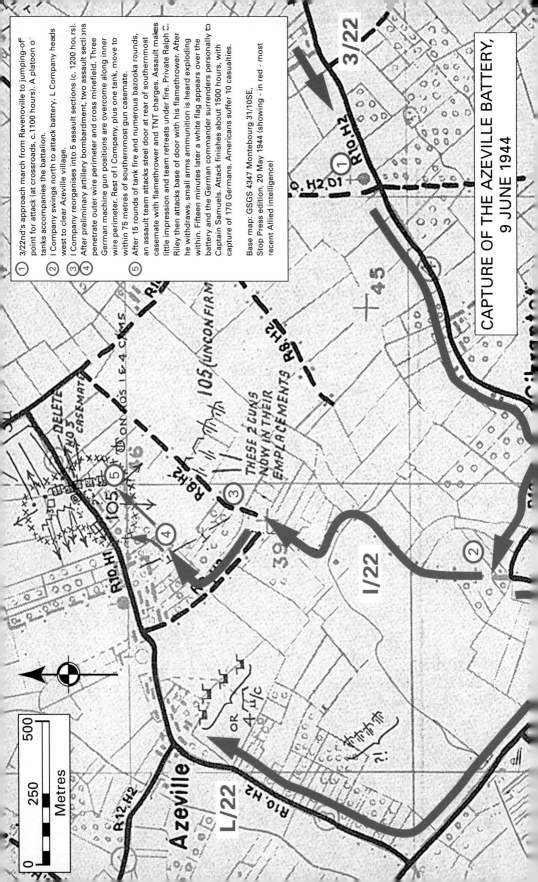

CAPTURE OF THE AZEVILLE BATTERY, 9 JUNE 1944

① 3/22nd's approach march from Ravenoville to jumping-off point for attack (at crossroads, c.1100 hours). A platoon of tanks accompanies the battalion.

② I Company swings north to attack battery. L Company heads west to clear Azeville village.

③ I Company reorganises into 5 assault sections (c. 1200 hours).

④ After preliminary artillery bombardment, two assault sections penetrate outer wire perimeter and cross minefield. Three German machine gun positions are overcome along inner wire perimeter. Rest of I Company, plus one tank, move to within 75 metres of southernmost gun casemate.

⑤ After 15 rounds of tank fire and numerous bazooka rounds, an assault team attacks steel door at rear of southernmost casemate with flamethrower and TNT charges. Assault makes little impression and team retreats under fire. Private Ralph Riley then attacks base of door with his flamethrower. After he withdraws, small arms ammunition is heard exploding within. Fifteen minutes later a white flag appears over the battery and the German commander surrenders personally to Captain Samuels. Attack finishes about 1500 hours, with capture of 170 Germans. Americans suffer 10 casualties.

Base map: GSGS 4347 Montebourg 31/10SE,
Stop Press edition, 20 May 1944 (showing - in red - most recent Allied intelligence)

3/22

1/22

L/22

Azeville

Metres
0   250   500

Azeville Battery

Renseignements Azeville et Crisbecq, La Batterie d'Azeville, 'Les Cruttes', 50310 Azeville; tel: +33 (0)6 63 11 60 20. Open daily 1400–1800 Apr–May, 1100–1800 June & Sept, 1100–1900 July & Aug, and 1400–1800 All Saints Day; groups by arrangement. Guided tours of the underground tunnel system beneath the battery. Admission charge; free parking.

erected in 1987 to mark the site of a temporary USAAF airfield. The inscription reads: 'Just after D-Day the Advanced Landing Ground A-7 was built on this site by the Ninth USA Air Force 365th Fighter Group. 28-06-1944 – 15-08-1944 – 21-09-1987'. Return southwards back down the D14 towards St-Marcouf, and turn right back onto the D69. (If you prefer not to visit this memorial, simply carry straight on along the D69 at the crossroads with the D14.)

Continue straight on the D69. After 1 km, turn left onto the D269, then after a further 1 km turn right towards Azeville (still on the D269 – the road straight on is the D420). The Azeville battery is on the D269 immediately before the village; parking is on the left hand side. One of the casemates (Number 4) is the museum for both the Azeville and Crisbecq batteries.

After looking round the site, stand in the car park facing southward, with Azeville village to your right. You are looking in the direction of the American attack which captured the battery on 9 June.

One of the casemates of the Azeville battery, now converted into the battery museum display. *(Author)*

BATTLEFIELD TOURS

One of the lesser gun positions at the Azeville battery showing the damage done in the American attacks to capture it. Photographed on 15 September. *(USNA)*

THE ACTION: The battery at Azeville consisted of four 105-mm Schneider guns in concrete casemates. The two casemates on the far side of the road were Type 650s, each topped by a 37-mm anti-aircraft gun position. All the casemates were linked by underground passages. The garrison of 170 men was commanded by *Oberleutnant* (Lieutenant) Kattning. There was no observation bunker since the coast cannot be seen from the battery position, so the Crisbecq battery acted as its observation and fire control.

Captain Joseph T. Samuels commanding I Company, 3/22nd Infantry Regiment, describes the capture of the Azeville battery on 9 June 1944.

'The one tank fired 15 rounds at the nearest large [casemate] pillbox and 3 assault sections began to work on the pillboxes. Bazookas and tank were ineffective, although penetrating the walls to some depth... The attack was concentrated against the back door of the first pillbox. One section discharged its flame thrower, and 2 pack charges [were] set off against the door. Then a satchel charge of 40 pounds of TNT was set off knocking our own man unconscious by the concussion, but the charge was ineffective. Captain Samuels then called for the flame thrower from another section. Private Ralph G. Riley reported and Samuels told him "All right Riley, go in and give it a few squirts". Riley crossed an open field, tried to discharge the flame thrower, which failed to ignite. He then lit it with a match and emptied the full tank under the door, dropped it and ran. His canteen and gas mask were full of holes when he returned. After this second dose the captain waited. Small arms fire began to pop inside. He waited several more minutes, and finally a white flag appeared... the battery commander [*Oberleutnant* Kattning] offering to surrender if the captain would order his men to cease firing. The captain obliged and 169 Germans filed out.'

Source: Combat Interviews, 4th Infantry Division, US National Archives.

TO CONCLUDE THE TOUR: Leave the Azeville battery and turn left towards Azeville. Take the left hand fork (still the D269) when leaving the village and continue for 1 km to the T-junction with the D115. Turn left and then go straight on for 3.5 km (ignoring turnings for minor roads and tracks, and the crossroads with the D15) to the crossroads with the D17, and turn right

The main command bunker of the Azeville battery, which now houses the battery museum. *(Author)*

towards St-Mère-Église. On the left after about 700 metres is the entrance to la Londe Farm, the site of the USAAF landing strip built on 11 June; about 700 metres beyond this also on the left is a memorial to 552nd AAA/AW Battalion which protected the airfield. Continue into Ste-Mère-Église and follow signposts to the A-13 to end the tour.

TO CONTINUE WITH TOUR D: Retrace your route from the Azeville battery via the D269 and the D69 to the crossroads with the D14, turn right onto the D14, go through St-Marcouf and straight on to Ravenoville. Either continue straight on for about 1.5 km to the German Prisoner of War Memorial Marker outside Foucarville (*see Stand D1*), or omit this and take a left turn onto D15 Robertson Road (*also described in Stand D1*) to begin the tour from there.

TOUR D

THE LANDING BEACHES

OBJECTIVE: This tour includes both the planned and actual sites of the Utah Beach landing on D-Day, together with the link-up between 101st Airborne Division and 4th Infantry Division at Exit 1 and Exit 2 from the beach. Utah Beach itself, with its museum and many memorials is a major centre for ceremonies commemorating the Battle of Normandy.

This tour could be done as a short tour of about half a day, but it is easily possible to spend an entire day at Utah Beach by itself, including combining the historical sights with enjoying the beach location. This tour could also be combined with either Tour B or Tour C over one or two days.

Stand D1: The LeClerc Monument

DIRECTIONS: Leave the A-13 at Ste-Mère-Église, taking the D17 northeast for 6 km through Beuzeville-au-Plain and Fournel to the T-junction with the D14 at Foucarville. This is the coastal ridge road, with hedgerows all around and the exit roads from

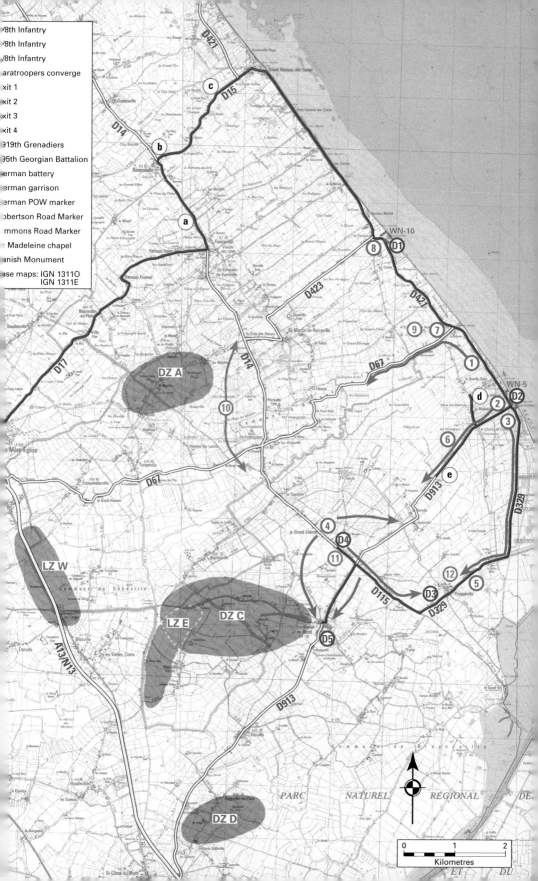

8th Infantry

8th Infantry

8th Infantry

aratroopers converge

xit 1

xit 2

xit 3

xit 4

919th Grenadiers

95th Georgian Battalion

erman battery

erman garrison

erman POW marker

obertson Road Marker

mmons Road Marker

Madeleine chapel

anish Monument

ase maps: IGN 1311O
         IGN 1311E

the sea on the east side, all of them tracks through the inundations in 1944. Turn left onto the D14 and on the left after about 100 metres is a German prisoner of war memorial marker, the site of Continental Central Enclosure Number 19. Established at the end of June 1944 and lasting until 1947, this camp housed 40,000 prisoners at its height and covered a considerable area of farmland. Carry straight on for just over 1 km to Ranouville. At the crossroads turn right onto the D15 towards the beach, note the signpost 'Robertson Road', and after about 1 km straight on note the signpost 'Simmons Road'. The D15 is the northernmost of the beach exit and coastal roads that have sections named in memory of US soldiers of 1st Engineer Special Brigade (1st ESB) killed in the Utah Beach battles or in clearing obstacles and ordnance. There are 43 of these road sections; most of the men commemorated are buried in the Normandy American Cemetery at Colleville-sur-Mer on Omaha Beach.

At Grand-Hameau-des-Dunes, turn right at the T-junction southwards onto the coast road D421. Note the resistance nest blockhouses. After 2 km just past D17 Leighton Road, note more resistance nest blockhouses, and the coastal road ridgeline on the right hand side. Go straight on for 2 km to the T-junction with the D423 Begel Road. This was Exit 4 from Utah Beach on D-Day. Just beyond on the left hand side is the LeClerc Monument, with a car park. Walk around the monument area.

The WN-10 resistance nest position (also known as WN-101) at Utah Beach near the LeClerc Monument. *(Author)*

Utah Beach on 9 June, showing the transformation of the beach into a supply base. *(USNA)*

THE ACTION: The LeClerc Monument is at les-Dunes-de-Varreville, part of Utah Beach as it was originally planned for D-Day, and later developed as the main area for disembarkation. The monument marks this as the place where the Fighting French 2nd Armoured Division came ashore in July 1944, commanded by Maj-Gen Jacques Philippe LeClerc (the Viscomte de Hautecloque, who took the war-name LeClerc to protect his family who had remained in German-occupied France). The inscription reads in French: 'On 6 June 1944 at Dawn the Allied Armies Landed Here – And Here First Landed General LeClerc Commander of 2nd Armoured Division'. There is a display board and marble memorial stones to the units of the division. The vehicles at the monument are an American-built M-3 half-track personnel carrier and M-8 scout car, both used to equip the division and painted in its formation signs. Monuments in a similar style can be found throughout Normandy, including one in the main square at Ste-Mère-Église and one outside the *hôtel de ville* at Carentan.

Walk to the beach and turn left. On top of the sand dunes after about 250 metres are bunkers of a resistance nest. In 1944 these bunkers extended further on either side of the beach exit. The entrance to one of these bunkers has at some point been marked with paint as 'W 10'. This fits with the records which show the site as the location of the resistance nest usually known as WN-10. Out to sea the remains of the Gooseberry blockships may still be visible.

View from the coast road inland close to the LeClerc Memorial, showing a German concrete bunker close to a modern building on the right, the flat water meadow, and the higher ground of the ridgeline in the distance. *(Author)*

Stand D2: Utah Beach

DIRECTIONS: Leave the LeClerc Monument, turn left and continue south on the D421 Fottrell Road for 2 km to the T-junction with D67 Blair Road, which was Exit 3 on D-Day. Continue on the D421, which for the next 2 km straight on to Utah Beach is named Route des Alliés. Utah Beach has an organised road system and signposted car park. The entire modern structure including the ceremonial platforms, a museum, and a restaurant, is built into or on top of the WN-5/WN-104 resistance nest. Walk round the site, ending on the beach.

THE SITE: Opened in 1962, the museum is partly funded by Ste-Marie-du-Mont local council. Outside as part of the museum are vehicles, guns and other equipment used in 1944, including

Utah Beach Landing Museum

Musée du Debarquement d'Utah Beach, Utah Beach, 50480
Ste-Marie-du-Mont. Tel: +33 (0)2 33 71 53 35; web: <www.utahbeach.org>
or <www.utah-beach.org>; email: <muse.utahbeach@wanadoo.fr>.
Open daily 0930–1900 May–Sept, 1000–1230 and 1400–1800 Apr and Oct,
otherwise 1000–1230 & 1400–1730 on weekends and public holidays.
Admission charge; free parking.

an LCVP. The museum has memorial plaques to 238th Engineer Combat Battalion and 406th Fighter Group, and a statue to US Sea Service Personnel.

Opposite the car park is the privately-owned *Le Roosevelt Café*, named after Teddy Roosevelt, which has a bunker captured on D-Day built into one side. A plaque on the side of the bunker identifies it as the site of the US Navy communications centre, manned by 41 men under Lieutenant W.B. MacDonald, part of 2nd Naval Beach Battalion, from 8 June until 31 October 1944. The café website <www.le-roosevelt.com> gives a description (in English) of the bunker and these men's experiences.

Prominent among the memorials is the 'KM 00' (for 'Kilometre 0.0') marker of the *Voie de la Liberté*, (Road to Liberty) to go with the 'Kilometre 0' outside the *hôtel de ville* at Ste-Mère-Église (*see Tour B*). These ceremonial stones mark the path of US Third Army under Lt Gen George S. Patton Jr., including 2nd French Armoured Division, from Utah Beach through France and into Belgium in 1944. There are four processional routes: from Ste-Mère-Église to Cherbourg; from Ste-Mère-Église to Avranches (at the base of the Cotentin), from Avranches to Metz, and from Metz to Bastogne in Belgium (focal point of the 'Battle of the Bulge' in December 1944). The symbolism of the marker stone is (from top to bottom): 48 stars for the states of the USA in 1944, rectangles in a different colour for each of the four routes, the marker number, the Torch of Liberty with the formation sign of Third Army on it, and waves representing the ocean. The inscription reads, in French: 'Here the American Armies Landed 6 June 1944'.

The main ceremonial viewing platform is built over a bunker. Markers on the platform show the direction and distance out to sea of the major Allied warships of Task Force U on D-Day. The red granite Liberation Memorial (Utah Beach US Federal Monument) was erected in 1984, with the inscription: 'This

Monument was Erected by the United States of America in Humble Tribute to its Sons Who Lost Their Lives in the Liberation of These Beaches 6 June 1944'. Beneath the platform is a bunker with a plaque to Maj Gen Eugene Mead Caffey (the deputy commander of 1st ESB as a colonel on D-Day, and later its commander) and the names of the dead of the brigade inscribed on the walls. There are individual monuments to 4th Infantry Division, 90th Infantry Division and 1st Engineer Special Brigade (with a list of all its units around the sides). There are also plaques to the US Coast Guard, and to 1st ESB HQ.

THE ACTION: Walk down the path through the sand dunes, marked as Rowe Road (note the plaque marking the Fiftieth Anniversary Ceremonies in 1994), and onto the beach. On the right on the beach side of the museum is a concrete mount for a French tank turret and 37-mm gun (sometimes under repair and replaced by a 50-mm anti-tank gun), and there are metal hedgehogs in the dunes.

> **Medal of Honor citation for Brig Gen Theodore Roosevelt Jr., assistant commander 4th Infantry Division, for his actions on 6 June 1944.**
>
> 'After two verbal requests to accompany the leading assault elements in the Normandy invasion had been denied, Brigadier General Roosevelt's written request for this mission was approved and he landed with the first wave of the forces assaulting the enemy-held beaches. He repeatedly led groups from the beach, over the seawall and established them inland. His valor, courage, and presence in the very front of the attack and his complete unconcern at being under heavy fire inspired the troops to heights of enthusiasm and self-sacrifice. Although the enemy had the beach under constant direct fire, Brigadier General Roosevelt moved from one locality to another, rallying men around him, directed and personally led them against the enemy. Under his seasoned, precise, calm, and unfaltering leadership, assault troops reduced beach strong points and rapidly moved inland with minimum casualties. He thus contributed substantially to the successful establishment of the beachhead in France.'
>
> *Source:* US Army Center for Military History.

The ceremony held at Utah Beach on 11 November 1944, led by Colonel Eugene M. Caffey, to unveil the memorial to 1st Engineer Special Brigade. *(USNA)*

1st Lieutenant John C. Rebarchek of E Company, 2/8th Infantry, describes landing on Utah Beach with the first wave on D-Day.

'Rebarchek said that he was confused for a little while after landing because he didn't know that he had landed too far to the south... He had landed south of the road on [Uncle] Red Beach. There was no small arms opposition on the beach. They did receive some rocket [*Nebelwerfer*] fire, he said, but in general there was almost no opposition. They waded in 100 yards of waist-deep water. When the men reached the dry beach they waved their rifles and shouted "Goddam, we're on French soil!" There was no opposition at the time. When they got across the dunes they began to see artillery fire directly in front of them. Rebarchek went back to the beach to pick up some of his men, and then led his section straight through the artillery barrage without losing a man.'

Source: Combat Interviews, 4th Infantry Division, US National Archives.

Captain George L. Maybry Jr. of 2/8th Infantry (later a Medal of Honor winner) describes his own actions moving off Utah Beach towards Exit 1 on D-Day.

'From the crack of bullets passing inches above his head, he was able to locate the enemy dug in on a sand dune about 100 yards to his front. Making a hasty survey of his position, he could see mines that had been uncovered by strong winds and shifting sand. He now knew that he was in a mine field. A definite decision must be made and quickly! Would it be advantageous to try a withdrawal to the beach with the possibility of hitting a mine or should he continue the advance towards the enemy position... Based upon previous training and remembering the necessity of contacting Company G, he elected to push through the mines and engage the enemy. The first rush forward directed at a shell hole was begun with good progress in spite of small arms fire; but upon the last leap for an inviting shell hole, his foot set off a mine. The explosion slammed him against the ground with a tremendous thud – no injuries from it – just shaken up a bit.'

Source: Theodore A. Wilson, *D-Day 1944*, pp. 233–4.

Le Roosevelt Café, showing the former German bunker built into its side. The apparent 'windows' on the bunker are painted on, reproduced from photographs showing its appearance when used by the Americans after D-Day. *(Author)*

Stand D3: Pouppeville

DIRECTIONS: Leave the Utah Beach carpark, at first taking the D913 Daniel Road directly inland towards Ste-Marie-du-Mont. This stretch of road was Exit 2 on D-Day and is lined with flagpoles for ceremonials. At the crossroads after 750 metres turn right, and then go straight on for another 300 metres. On the right is the chapel of la Madeleine, rebuilt after the war with a stained glass window memorial to the Fighting French (known as the Free French between 1940 and 1944). Return to the crossroads with the D913 and turn right again towards Ste-Marie-du-Mont. This stretch of the D913 is called Hinkel Road. After 1.2 km on the left hand side is a statue and memorial, with parking, to 800 Danish sailors who took part in the D-Day landings at Utah Beach.

The chapel at la Madeleine, repaired and rebuilt since 1944. *(Author)*

Retracing your route, return back down the D913 to Utah Beach and turn right southwards onto the D421, which turns inland becoming the D329 Ham Road, which was the track leading to Exit 1 on D-Day. On the left is the bird sanctuary. Go straight on for 2.5 km to the T-junction, take the right fork, still the D329 but now Effler Road, for 1.5 km to Pouppeville. Drive through the village and carry on for about 250 metres. Park and stand looking back down the D329 through the village.

Part of the Exit 1 route from Utah Beach to Pouppeville (the D329 MacGowan Road). The sign identifies this as part of the Regional Nature Reserve. *(Author)*

THE ACTION: It was here that 2/8th Infantry from Utah Beach achieved the first link-up of D-Day with troops from 101st Airborne.

Lieutenant Luther Knowlton of 101st Airborne Division describes the link up with 4th Infantry Division at Pouppeville on D-Day.

'Nothing was moving on the causeway until a tank came grinding round the bend about 250 yards beyond the last building. In the reeds overlooking the entrance to the hamlet, waited men of the 4th Infantry Division's 8th Infantry Regiment who had heard the fire fight going on. They were not observed by the Airborne soldiers. The tank approached slowly up the narrow road. Its identity was unknown. One of our men fired his machine gun from the shelter of a stone wall. The bullets ricocheted off the heavy armour plating. He was not taking any chances.'

Source: George E. Koskimaki, *D-Day with the Screaming Eagles*, p. 175.

The tank stopped and displayed an orange recognition panel. Lieutenant Knowlton replied with an orange smoke grenade. An officer of 4th Infantry Division stepped forward from the reeds to shake hands with Knowlton; it was Captain Maybry (quoted above), who had recovered from his earlier near-miss in the minefield and had led the advance. He was taken to meet Maj Gen Taylor.

Stand D4: Brécourt

DIRECTIONS: Go straight on from Pouppeville to the T-junction with the D115/D14, the coastal ridge road. Turn right onto what is now the D14 Fitts Road for about 1.6 km to the crossroads with D913 Sonnier Road, and then go straight on for a further 500 metres to a crossroads with a minor road; the left hand turn here leads to the Manoir du Brécourt (note signpost to Brécourt). Stay on the main road, pull over and park when safe.

The crossroads of the D14 with the minor road leading to Brécourt. The fields to the left of this picture were the site of the German battery position captured by the American paratroopers on D-Day. *(Author)*

THE ACTION: In the fields on the left hand side towards Brécourt was a German battery of four 105-mm guns. The guns were not fixed and the defences were made entirely of earth and timber, so nothing remains of the position. This is the location of an episode made famous by Stephen Ambrose's best selling book *Band of Brothers* and the television mini-series made from it (2001), relating the experiences of E Company, 2/506th PIR.

Defended by about 50 soldiers, probably of II/191st Artillery Regiment, the battery opened fire on Utah Beach at 0700 hours. Commanded by Lieutenant Richard (Dick) Winters, E Company was temporarily reduced to twelve men following the night parachute landings. At 0830 hours, Winters led his men in an attack on the position that lasted for three hours and resulted in its capture for the loss of four American dead and two wounded.

Sergeant Carwood Lipton, E Company, 2/506th PIR, describes the attack on the battery at Brécourt on D-Day.

'We fought as a team without standout stars. We were like a machine. We didn't have anyone who leapt up and charged a machine gun. We knocked it out or made it withdraw by manoeuvre and teamwork or mortar fire. We were smart, there weren't many flashy heroics. We had learned that heroics was the way to get killed without getting the job done, and getting the job done was more important... It was the high morale of the E Company men, the quickness and the audacity of the frontal attack, and the fire into their positions from several different directions that demoralised the German force and convinced them that they were being hit by a much larger force.'

Source: Stephen Ambrose, *Band of Brothers*, pp. 79 & 83.

The fields at Brécourt that were the location for the German battery captured by E Company, 506th PIR, on D-Day. *(Author)*

Lieutenant Winters was recommended for the Medal of Honor and was awarded the Distinguished Service Cross. All twelve members of the company who took part in the attack received decorations; Sergeant Lipton received the Bronze Star.

Stand D5: Sainte-Marie-du-Mont

DIRECTIONS: Return to the crossroads and turn right onto the D913 Sonnier Road, go straight on into the centre of Ste-Marie-du-Mont. Park in or near the main square. Walk around the village and end in the square facing the west end of the church.

Ste-Marie-du-Mont with its distinctive church tower, as seen approaching from the sea along the D913, which in 1944 was Exit 2 from Utah Beach. *(Author)*

THE ACTION: The ornate church tower made a distinctive landmark against the dawn on D-Day, identifying the village and helping American paratroopers locate themselves. In the main square on the *mairie* (mayor's office) is a plaque in English and French: 'To Pay Tribute to the Soldiers of the 101st American Airborne Division Who Liberated Our Village at Dawn on June 6th 1944', and next to it a *Voie de la Liberté* marker (Number 7 on the D913). There is a 'D-Day Trail' of placards fixed to houses and other locations in the village describing (in French) the events of its liberation. The placard fixed to the *mairie* is Number 5, describing a shoot-out that took place in the square at dawn between an American paratrooper and a German soldier.

The main square at Ste-Marie-du-Mont on 7 June, looking westward from the church. The memorial to the village losses of the First World War is to the right of the picture. *(USNA)*

The main square at Ste-Marie-du-Mont today. The church is on the left of the picture. The memorial to the losses of the First World War, with a metal statue placed on the memorial stone, is visible on the far side of the square. The building to the right of the picture has a placard from the village D-Day Trail in front of it. *(Author)*

Signposts indicating a museum refer to the *Musée du Débarquement d'Utah Beach* (described above).

Ste-Marie-du-Mont was the D-Day objective for E Company, 2/506th PIR, and a photograph reproduced in Ambrose's book shows men of E Company posed in the main square on 7 June. With so much scattering of the paratroopers the village was captured not by any one unit but by a mixture of individuals from 101st Airborne and 4th Infantry Divisions.

TO CONCLUDE THE TOUR: Leave Ste-Marie-du-Mont and continue straight on westward along the D913 through Vierville towards St-Côme-du-Mont and the A-13. This road was the main axis of advance for the German I/6th Paratroop Regiment on the evening of D-Day, and for men of 101st Airborne in the opposite direction on 7–8 June. As you leave Ste-Marie-du-Mont, Drop Zone C and Landing Zone E are the high ground on the right. After passing through Vierville, Drop Zone D and Angouville-au-Plain village are below the ridgeline on the left.

TO CONTINUE WITH TOUR A: Leave Ste-Marie-du-Mont by the D70 north-westerly towards les Forges and Chef-du-Pont.

TO CONTINUE WITH E: Leave Ste-Marie-du-Mont by the D913 towards Angouville-au-Plain.

The church at Vierville, showing repairs from damage inflicted in 1944. *(Author)*

TOUR E

THE CARENTAN CAUSEWAY

OBJECTIVE: This tour looks at the capture of Carentan by troops of 101st Airborne Division during 7–12 June. This part of the battlefield has been changed considerably by building developments since 1945, particularly the urban spread of Carentan and creation of an industrial zone to the west, the building of the D971 road as a by-pass on the western side of the town, and the A-13 autoroute by-passing it to the north and east. The River Taute downstream from Carentan has been canalised as the Canal de Carentan de la Mer, and the bridges opposite Brévands no longer exist. The la Barquette lock is very difficult to reach, and although it is visible in passing from the A-13, due caution should always be taken when driving. Consequently, this tour is intended as a half-day or less, to give some experience of the Carentan battle and possibly as a way of rounding off a longer touring day. It fits well carrying on from either Tour B or Tour D.

Stand E1: Angouville-au-Plain

DIRECTIONS: From the A-13 take the D913 towards Ste-Marie-du-Mont. After 1.3 km at the crossroads with the D913E turn right into Angouville-au-Plain. There is parking space in the village centre next to the church, and nearby a memorial stone to Privates Robert E. Wright and Kenneth J. Moore, medics of 2/501st PIR: 'For Humane and Life Saving Care Rendered to 80 Combatants and A Child in This Church In June 1944'. Stand facing this stone, looking east, with the church on your left.

THE ACTION: The counterattack by 6th Paratroop Regiment on the evening of D-Day came from behind you, with the Americans defending falling back, and then counter-attacking from your front on 7 June to clear the village. The small hamlet of les Droueries is 1.2 km directly behind you, close to la Haute-Addeville and la Basse-Addeville.

When the attack by 6th Paratroop Regiment captured the

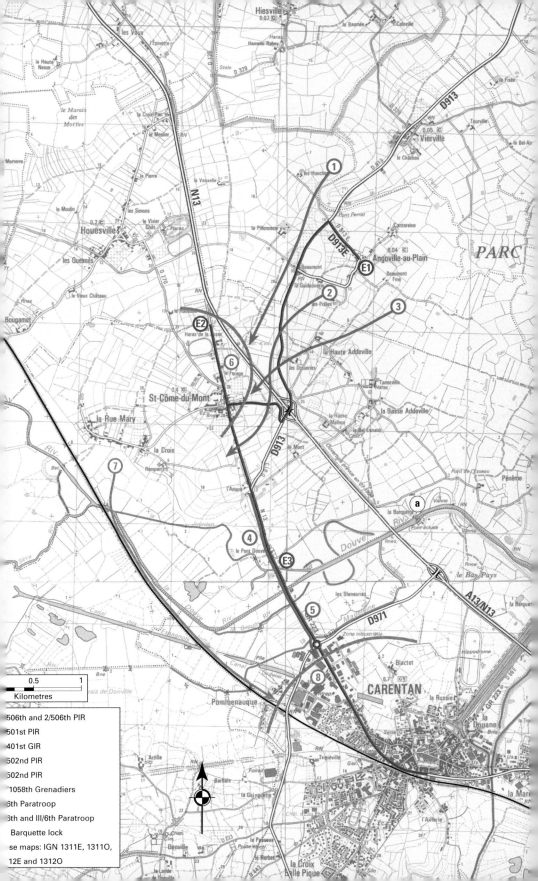

Hiesville
0.07 [C]

les Vaux
l'Epinette

la Baumée
Caloville

la Haute
Nesse

le Messier
la Croix-Pan

Vierville
le Château

le Bel-Air
la Fisée

D 913

RN 0.05 [C]
Tourville

Morterre

le Moulin

les Simons
le Vivier
Chât.

la Pierre

la Vauxelle

les Houches ①

le Grand Vey
RN
Pont Perrat
Canterene

0.2 [C]
Houesville

les Quesnils

le Vieux Châte.

PARC

D 913 E

Angoville-au-Plain
0.04 [C]

E1

Beaumont
la Guidonnerie

Beaumont
Fme

② les Prèles

③

le Vieux Château

E2
Haras de la

⑥
le Ferage

la Haute Addeville

les Doueries

Tamerville
Haras

la Basse Addeville

St-Côme-du-Mont
0.4 [C]

la Haute
Maison

la Bel Esnault
Chât.

la Rue Mary

la Croix

D 913

le Mont

Pont de l'Esseau
Pénême

Ramparts

l'Amont

⑦

a
la Barquette

Vanne

Douve River

Pont-écluse
Vanne

④
le Pont Douve

Jobrdan

RN

E3

le Bas Pays

les Bleneuries

A13/N13

le Barque

Canal de

⑤

Madeleine

D 971

Zone Industrielle

Blactot

marais de Donville

Canal des Espagnols

⑧

Serre

CARENTAN
8.7 [C]

la Russie

Hippodrome

la Douane

0.5   1
Kilometres

Pommenauque

Pile

la Mare

506th and 2/506th PIR
501st PIR
401st GIR
502nd PIR
502nd PIR
1058th Grenadiers
6th Paratroop
6th and III/6th Paratroop
Barquette lock
se maps: IGN 1311E, 1311O,
12E and 1312O

Artille

Barbais

la Guinguette

Triéville

la Croix
Belle Pique

Benville

church late on D-Day, Privates Moore and Wright stayed with the wounded.

Private First Class Kenneth J. Moore, 2/501st PIR, recalls D-Day at Angouville-au-Plain church.

'Private Robert Wright and I were the only medics [out of sixteen in the battalion] to assemble with the 2nd Battalion at Angouville-au-Plain and les Droueries. During the day we assembled 75 casualties in the church... At dusk on D-Day, we were told our troops could not hold the church. We both stayed with the wounded and shortly after that, the Germans came into the church. An officer asked if we would care for their wounded also till we could be evacuated. We agreed and the German officer left. During the night the churchyard was a battleground. Two of our men died during the night. At dawn an American tank appeared outside the church and fired through the windows with machine guns. We displayed [orange recognition] panels and contacted the troops. They were 506th people and armor from the beach.'

Source: George E. Koskimaki, *D-Day with the Screaming Eagles*, p. 362.

Stand E2: St-Côme-du-Mont

DIRECTIONS: Leave the village retracing your route on the D913E, and turn left onto the D913 towards St-Côme-du-Mont. On the left is Drop Zone D for 101st Airborne Division, and the views on both sides still give a good idea of the terrain fought over in 1944. The D913 crosses by a flyover over the A-13. At the crossroads with the N13 (the old Cherbourg road) turn right into St-Côme-du-Mont. The road goes straight on through the village; the church on the left has some car parking space if needed. Continue straight on through the village, either driving or walking. The road has been blocked to traffic as a dead end 600 metres further on, but there is room to park and turn. Stand facing northwards, looking down the blocked section of the N13. Despite the A-13 cutting across the battlefield, this position gives an excellent view to the right of the battlefield from the D913 to the River Taute, and the mixture of hedgerows and orchards with water meadows that were marshland in 1944.

The area of Stand E2 at St-Côme-du-Mont on the blocked N13, looking north-eastwards. The A-13 autoroute is in the immediate foreground, with the hedgerow country stretching away east in the distance. *(Author)*

The blocked section of the N13 at St-Côme-du-Mont, taken from beyond the traffic barrier, looking north. This disused section gives some idea of how parts of the road would have looked in 1944. *(Author)*

THE ACTION: At about 1100 hours on D-Day, *Major* von der Heydte, commanding 6th Paratroop Regiment, rode a motorcycle to St-Côme-du-Mont and climbed up inside the church tower to get a view of the Utah Beach landings. What he saw led him to plan his counter-attack which took place that evening.

> *Major* **Friedrich Frieherr von der Heydte describes his view from St-Côme-du-Mont church tower at 1100 hours on D-Day.**
>
> 'An overwhelming picture presented itself to [myself as] the regimental commander from the church tower of St-Côme-du-Mont. Before [me] lay the coast and the sea. The horizon was strewn with hundreds of ships and countless landing boats and barges were moving back and forth between the ships and the shore, landing troops and tanks. It was an almost peaceful picture... The noise of battle could not be heard, and from the church tower of St-Côme-du-Mont there was no sign of German defence activities. Only a shot rang out here and there whenever the sentries of the German battalions came in contact with Allied paratroopers.'
>
> *Source:* David C. Isby, *Fighting the Invasion*, pp. 227–8.

The twelfth century church at St-Côme-du-Mont. It was from this church tower that *Major* von der Heydte watched the morning landings at Utah Beach. *(Author)*

St-Côme-du-Mont was held by III/1058th Grenadiers on
6–8 June, forming a defensive arc to your right. The attack by
101st Airborne under Colonel Sink that captured the village on
8 June came from your right down the D913 from Vierville and
Angouville-au-Plain.

Women from Carentan place flowers on the temporary grave of an American
soldier who has been buried where he fell, 19 June. *(USNA)*

Stand E3: The Carentan Causeway

DIRECTIONS: Retrace your route on the N13, and go straight
on down the hill from St-Côme-du-Mont towards Carentan. The
view from the south side of the village across the plain gives a
good idea of conditions in 1944. Once on the plain, along the
N13 causeway road there are picnic spots and benches with
parking. Pull over at the one of these just past the hamlet of
le Pont-Douve and just before the River Jourdan. Stand looking
along the road towards Carentan. La Barquette lock is on the
River Douve about 1.2 km to your left.

The centre of modern Carentan. The church spire is visible in the background. *(Author)*

The liberation memorial to the 101st Airborne Division close to the *hôtel de ville* in Carentan. *(Author)*

The main church at Carentan as it appears today. *(Author)*

THE ACTION: It was along this causeway that 502nd PIR advanced on 10–11 June in an effort to reach Carentan against the defenders of 6th Paratroop Regiment.

> **Medal of Honor citation for Lt Col Robert G. Cole, commanding 3/502nd PIR, for his actions on 11 June 1944.**
>
> 'Lieutenant Colonel Cole was personally leading his battalion in forcing the last four bridges on the road to Carentan when his entire unit was suddenly pinned to the ground by intense and withering enemy rifle, machinegun, mortar, and artillery fire placed upon them from well-prepared and heavily fortified positions within 150 yards of the foremost elements. After the devastating and unceasing enemy fire had for over one hour prevented any move and inflicted numerous casualties, Lieutenant Colonel Cole, observing this almost hopeless situation, courageously issued orders to assault the enemy positions with fixed bayonets. With utter disregard for his own safety and completely ignoring the enemy fire, he rose to his feet in front of his battalion and with drawn pistol shouted to his men to follow him in the assault. Catching up a fallen man's rifle and bayonet, he charged on and led

BATTLEFIELD TOURS

the remnants of his battalion across the bullet-swept open ground and into the enemy position. His heroic and valiant action in so inspiring his men resulted in the complete establishment of our bridgehead across the Douve River. The cool fearlessness, personal bravery, and outstanding leadership displayed by Lieutenant Colonel Cole reflect great credit upon himself and are worthy of the highest praise in the military service.'

Source: US Army Center for Military History.

Continue straight on along the N13. The final bridge of the four over the River Madeleine is immediately before a large roundabout marking the junction of the N13 with the D971. Continue into the centre of Carentan, which is a pleasant town with many cafés and other places to rest at the end of a tour, as well as tourist shops. Outside the *hôtel de ville* (town hall) is a column in the same style as the LeClerc Monument (*see Tour D*) with the inscription, in French: 'The Heroism of the Allied Forces Liberated Europe – On 12 June 1944 the 101st Airborne Division Opened the Glorious Road to Victory'. At the base of the column is a plaque placed by the 101st Airborne Division Association.

TO END THE TOUR: Follow signs to the A-13.

The town centre of Carentan, showing the memorial to the French dead of the First World War. *(Author)*

ON YOUR
RETURN

FURTHER RESEARCH

If you are coming back to Great Britain, even if only staying for a short time, then you may want to read and find out more about the battle once you return. The airborne forces in particular have attracted considerable attention for their achievements. The first point of call for many people will probably be a website. Many of these are very good indeed, but please remember that anyone can put anything on a website, and they are not always completely accurate. Of the websites listed in this book, that of the Airborne Museum at Ste-Mère-Église <www.Airborne-museum.org>, which is available in both French and English, is good and has excellent links to other reliable websites. In addition, the major American units that took part in the battle have their own websites with useful links to others.

4th Infantry Division: www.4thinfantry.org/home.html

82nd Airborne Division: www.bragg.army.mil/www-82DV

90th Infantry Division: www.grunts.net/army/90thid.html

101st Airborne Division: www.chesapeake.net/~fuzz

DC-3/Dakota Historical Society:

   www.dc3history.org/dc3_historicalsociety.htm

The US Army Center of Military History: www.army.mil/cmh-pg has much material available on its website including the US Army official history of the Normandy landings, *Cross Channel Attack*.

Most of the material used in preparing this book came from either published official sources or from documents in the US National Archives or the National Archives of Great Britain, or from published personal accounts. Of particular value were the combat interviews undertaken with the airborne forces by the team under Colonel S.L.A. Marshall in July 1944, which formed the basis of his own book *Night Drop*. The present author only regrets that he could not include more of these remarkable stories in this account, along with the stories of men from both sides who fought in other units. But there is no shortage of books dealing with various aspects of the battle, and telling the stories of the men who fought it. The following were the most useful in writing this book.

Above: The Îles St-Marcouf viewed from Utah Beach. *(Jonathan Falconer)*

Page 185: Amphibious vehicles of 470th Amphibious Truck Company, part of 1st Engineer Special Brigade, landing supplies at Utah Beach on 8 June. *(USNA)*

German Order of Battle 1944: The Directory, Prepared by Allied Intelligence, of Regiments, Formations and Units of the German Armed Forces; London, Greenhill, 1994.

Operation 'Neptune': The Landings in Normandy 6th June 1944, British Naval Staff History Battle Summary Number 39, 1952; reprinted London, HMSO, 1994.

Utah Beach to Cherbourg (6 June – 27 June 1944), American Forces in Action Series, Historical Division, Department of the Army; Washington DC, The Center of Military History, US Army, 1947.

Stephen E. Ambrose, *Band of Brothers: E Company, 506th Regiment, 101st Airborne, From Normandy to Hitler's Eagle's Nest*; New York, Touchstone, 1992.

Stephen E. Ambrose, *D-Day: June 6, 1944, The Battle for the Normandy Beaches*; New York, Simon & Schuster, 1994.

Mark A. Bando, *The 101st Airborne at Normandy*; Osceola, WI, Motorbooks International, 1994.

William B. Breuer, *Hitler's Fortress Cherbourg: The Conquest of a Bastion*; Briarcliff Manor, NY, Stein and Day, 1984.

David Chandler and James Lawton Collins (eds.), *The D-Day Encyclopedia*; New York, Simon and Schuster, 1994.

Napier Crookenden, *Dropzone Normandy*; Abingdon, Purnell, 1976.

Philippe Esvelin, *D-Day Gliders: Les Planeurs Américains du Jour J*; Bayeux, Heimdal, 2001.

Dominique François, *The 508th Parachute Infantry Regiment*; Valognes, Le Révérend, 2001.

Dominique François, *The 507th Parachute Infantry Regiment*; Valognes, Le Révérend, 2000.

Jonathan Gawne, *Spearheading D-Day: American Special Units of the Normandy Invasion*; Paris, Histoire & Collections, 2001.

Gordon A. Harrison, *Cross Channel Attack*, United States Army in World War II, The European Theater of Operations; Washington DC, The Center of Military History United States Army, 1951.

David C. Isby (ed.), *Fighting in Normandy: The German Army from D-Day to Villers-Bocage*; London, Greenhill, 2001.

David C. Isby (ed.), *Fighting the Invasion: The German Army at D-Day*; London, Greenhill, 2000.

Robert J. Kershaw, *D-Day: Piercing the Atlantic Wall*; Shepperton, Ian Allan, 1993.

George E. Koskimaki, *D-Day with the Screaming Eagles*; New York, Vantage, 1970.

S.L.A. Marshall, *Night Drop: The American Airborne Invasion of Normandy*; New York, Little, Brown, 1962.

Samuel W. Mitcham, *Hitler's Legions: The German Order of Battle in World War II*; London, Leo Cooper, 1985.

Alexandre Renaud, *Sainte-Mère-Église*; Paris, Julliard, 1984.

Cornelius Ryan, *The Longest Day: The D-Day Story*; London, Victor Gollancz, 1982.

Anthony Saunders, *Hitler's Atlantic Wall*; Thrupp, Sutton, 2001.

Deryk Wills, *Put on Your Boots and Parachutes!*; Leicester, privately published, 1992.

Theodore A. Wilson (ed.), *D-Day 1944*; Abilene, KA, University Press of Kansas, 1971.

Niklas Zetterling, *Normandy 1944: German Military Organisation, Combat Power and Organizational Effectiveness*; J.J. Fedorowicz, Winnipeg, 2000.

Most of these books would be available only from specialist libraries or through inter-library loan. In Great Britain, good starting places for any study of the battle of Normandy are the Imperial War Museum, Lambeth Road, London SE1 6HZ; tel: 020 7416 5320; web: <www.iwm.org.uk>; and the D-Day Museum and Overlord Embroidery, Clarence Esplanade, Southsea PO5 2NT; tel: 023 9282 7261; web: <www.ddaymuseum.co.uk>.

INDEX

Page numbers in *italics* denote an illustration.

Advanced Landing Ground A-7 157
aircraft:-
Allied:
Airspeed Horsa *71*, *84*, 86, *86*, 88
C-47 Skytrain (Dakota DC-3) 43, 44, 45, 49, *50*, 55, 69, 86–7, *86*, 137
CG-4A Waco 69–70, 86–7, 88, 137, 147–8, *147*, *148*
de Havilland Mosquito 99
Lockheed P-38 Lightning 57
Martin B-26 Marauder 66
Republic P-47 Thunderbolt 57, 100
Short Stirline 44
Supermarine Spitfire 57, 66
German:
Heinkel 111 107
Junkers 52 107
Angouville-au-Plain 86, 98, 176, 178
armoured vehicles:-
Allied:
armoured bulldozer 62, 74, *80*
M4 Sherman 61, 62, 67, 68, *81*, 84, 100, 170
M7 Priest 61, *65*, 66, 75
M10 Wolverine 81, 100, 108
German/in German service:
Renault FT17 35, 166
Renault R35 39, *39*, 53, 77, 100
Panzer III 39
artillery:-
Allied:
57-mm anti-tank gun 69, 70, 87
155-mm gun 96
howitzers 51, 86, 87
German:
50-mm anti-tank gun *1*, *34*, 35, 38, 66, 154, 166
76.2-mm howitzer 38
88-mm gun 35, 66, 67, 69, 105, 107
105-mm Schneider 37, 38, 58, *101*, 171
122-mm gun 38, 69, 142
210-mm Skoda 37, 75, *102–3*, *113*, 154, *155*
anti-aircraft guns 154, 158
coastal batteries 24, 37, 99
Nebelwerfer 38, 91, 167

Atlantic Wall 20, *21*, 30–1, 34–6, *36*, *114*, 149–60
Audoville-la-Hubert 27, 50, 74, 80, 82
Azeville 37, 62, 94, 100, *101*, 155–9, *157*, *158*, *159*

Barnett, USS 55, 56
Barquette, la 26, 28, 40, 46, 71, 98
Barton, Maj Gen R.O. 76, 83
Bayfield, USS 41, 55
Belgian gates 35, 106
bocage 27, 28, *82*, 92, 150
Bradley, Lt Gen Omar 17, 88, 90, 104
Brandenberger, Lt Elmer 144
Brannen, Capt Malcolm 52
Brécourt 171–2, *171*, *172*
Brévands 26, 31, 70, 106
British Army: 10th (Inter-Allied) Commando 151
Burt, Pte W. 144, 145, 146
Butler, 2nd Lt John M. 147

Caffey, Col E.M. 76, 166, *167*
Camien, Pte John 145
Carentan 24, 39, 40, 41, 54, 88, 96, 104–10, *105*, *107*, 176–84, *182*, *183*, *184*
Cassidy, Lt Col 'Pat' 72, 142
Cauquigny 77, 96, 131–2, *132*
Chappuis, Lt Col Steve 71
Chef-du-Pont 28, 40, 41, *54*, 70, 78, 93, *117*, *122*, 123, 125–6, *125*, *127*, 130
Cherbourg 12, 14, 89, 90, 98, 100
Chicago Mission 69, 147–9
Cole, Lt Col Robert 71, 80, 108, 1830–4
Collier, Col John H. 109
Collins, Maj Gen J. Lawton 12, 55, 104
Combined Operations Pilotage Parties 24
Corry, USS 62, 75
Creek, Capt Roy E. 78, 123, *125*, 126
Crisbecq 37, *38*, 56, 62, 75, 94, 100, *102–3*, 104, *113*, 151, 153–5, *153*, *154*, *155*
Crouch, Lt Col Joel 44

Dollmann, *GenOb* Friedrich 14
Douve, River *21*, 24, 28, 41, 47, 50, 108
Dunes de Varreville, les 68, 91, 162–4
Dunn, Lt Col Edward C. 57

E-boat flotillas 14, 56, 84, 99
Eisenhower, Gen D.D. 16, 42, *42*

Ekman, Col William 78
Empire Gauntlet LSI(L) 55, 57
Enterprise, HMS 62
Ewell, Lt Col Julian 79

Falley, *GenLt* Wilhelm 43, 52
Fière, Manoir de la 28, 29, *29*, 40, 70, 77, 78, 96, 128–30, *129*
Fitch, USS 62
flooded areas 26, 28–9, 46, 71, *119*, *130*, *131*
Fontenay-sur-Mer 37, 62, 96
Forges, les 76, 83, 84, 87, 123
Foucarville 30, *34*, 37, *64*, 72, 77, 160
Free French Army: 2nd Armoured Division 163, 165

Gauthier, Lt Sims S 67
Gavin, Brig Gen James 47, 77, 78, 125, 128, 129–30, 137
German Army:-
Seventh Army 14, 20, 29, 43, 53, 71, 86, 98
Corps:
II Paratroop Corps 29
LXXXIV Corps 14, 29, 51, 53, 54, 93, 98, 104, 105
Divisions:
17th SS Pzgren *Götz von Berlichingen* 108–9
77th Inf 97
91st Airlanding 29, 39, 40, 43, 51, 53, 96, 97, 99
243rd Inf 29, 85, 91, 100, 104
352nd Inf 31, 51, 54
709th Inf 20, 29, 30, 39, 96, 104
Battlegroups etc.:
Artillery Group *Montebourg* 100
B'group *Hellmich* 104
B'group *Keil* 96, 150–1
B'group *Meyer* 54
B'group *Müller* 91, 92, 96
B'group *Rohrbach* 96, 151
B'group *Schlieben* 104
Regiments:
6th Paratroop 29, 39, 40, 51, 54, 85, 86, 87–8, 97–8, 105, 106–7, 108, 109, 176, 183
37th SS Pzgren 109
38th SS Pzgren 109
101st Fortress Rocket Projector 91, 100
191st Artillery 37, 38, 80, 85, 87, 172
243rd Artillery 91, 100
729th Gren 30–1, 91, 96
739th Gren 30–1, 96
914th Gren 31

German Army – Regts *cont.*
915th Gren 54
919th Gren 30, 35, 38, 43, 94, 136
920th Gren 91, 96, 151
921st Gren 29, 100
922nd Gren 29, 91, 92, 94, 96, 100
1049th Gren 97
1050th Gren 97
1057th Gren 44, 53, 77, 78, 84, 96, 125, 127, 129
1058th Gren 39, 53–4, 71, 72, 78, 79, 83, 85, 91, 92–3, 96, 98, 140–1, 181
1261st Coastal Artillery 36, 37, 37–8, 62, 69, 71, 75, 98, 142, 154
1262nd Coastal Artillery 36, 98
1709th Artillery 36
Battalions:
7th Army Assault 38, 51, 53–4, 83, 91, 92, 93, 94
17th SS Assault Gun 109
100th Panzer T/R 39, 53, 79, 84, 129
206th Panzer 39
243rd Engineer 91
352nd Fusilier 54
439th *Ost* 108
456th Artillery 91, 100
457th Artillery 91, 100
709th Anti-Tank 31, 91, 93
795th (Georgian) *Ost* 31, 51, 71, 79, 82, 83, 92, 94, 123, 146
Ost Battalions 20, 71, 105, 108
Volksdeutsche Battalions 21
German prisoners *3*, 76, 80, 92, 93, 98
Glennon, USS 99
Gooseberry breakwater 90, 164
Gorder, Capt Van 149
Grande Dune, la 24, 31, 68

Heydte, *Maj* von der 85, 86, 87, 108, 180
Hill 30 24, 77, 96, 108, 109, 126–8, *127*
Hitler, Adolf 13, 89, 108, 110

Îles St-Marcouf *20*, 21, *57*, 153, *187*
Iron Mike statue 128, *129*

Jahnke, *Leutnant* Arthur 35, 67, 68, 76
Johnson, Col Howard 70, 85, 86
Joseph T. Dickman, USS 55, 72

Kattning, *Oberlt* 158, 159

Keil, *Oberstlt* Günther 150–1
Kellam, Maj Frederick 130
Kerr, Col James E. 81
Knowlton, Lt Luther 170–1
König, *Oberst* Eugen 52
Krause, Lt Col Edward 78, 79, 139, 139–40

Landing Craft:
Control (LCC) 61, 67
Flak (LCF) 61
Gun (LCG) 61, 66
Headquarters (LCH) *56*
Mechanised (LCM) 60
Tank (LCT) 3, 42, *56*, 60, 61, 66, 67, 68, *121*
Vehicle Personnel (LCVP) *13*, 55, 60, 62, 66, 67, 165
Landing Ships, Tank (LST) *57*, 84, 90
LeClerc, Maj Gen Jacques Philippe 163
Leroux, Louis 29
Lillyman, Capt Frank L. 44
Linn, Maj Herschel 62, 73
Lipton, Sgt Carwood 172–3
Londe, la 100, 160
Luftwaffe: Third Air Fleet 15, 56, 82, 99, 107
Lutz, Pte Joe 127

McDonald, Lt W.B. 165
MacNeely, Lt Col Carlton 62
Madeleine, la 34, 68, 74, 169, *169*
Madeleine, River 106, 108, 184
Maloney, Lt Col A. 125, 130
Marcks, *Gen der Art* Erich 14, 43, 98, 104, 109, 151
Marshall, Col S.L.A. 144–5, 186
Maybry, Capt George L., Jr 168, 171
Merderet, River 28, *29*, 40, 41, 47, 50, *54*, 77, 96, *125*, *127*, 131–2
Meredith, USS 99
Messerschmidt, *Maj* Hugo 53
Minister, HMS 99
Montebourg 28, 39, 41, 88, 91, 100
Moore, Pte Kenneth J 176, 177
Murphy, Lt Col 'Mike' 147–8

Nelson, USS 99
Neuville-au-Plain 70, 78, 93, 96, 140–1, *141*
Nevada, USS 62
Nickrent, Staff Sgt Roy 146

Ohmsen, *Oblt-z-See* Walter 154
OKW (*Oberkommando der Wehrmacht*) 13, 89, 100, 154
Ostberg, Lt Col Edwin J. 125

Ostendorff, *SS-Gruppenführer* Werner 109

Patton, Lt Gen George S. 165
Peterson, Lt Cdr Herbert 62
Plaudo, Pte Charles R. *47*
Poole, Lt Noel 43
Pouppeville 27, *27*, 71, 74, 79–80, 80, 83, 100, 169–71, *170*
Pratt, Brig Gen Donald F. 70, 146–7
President Roosevelt, SS 55, 72

Quincy, USS 62, 85
Quinéville 21, 25, 28, 30, 31, 37, 41, 75, 76, 88, 104, 150–3, *150*; Museum of Liberty 151

Raff, Col Edison D. 84
Rebarchek, 1st Lt John C. 167
Renaud, Alexandre 43, *87*, 133–4
resistance nests:
WN-5/104 *1*, 31, 34, 35, 66–7, *67*, 68–9, 75, 76, *86*, 94, *162*, 164
WN-10/101 94, *162*, 164
Rich, USS 99
Ricker, Lt John B. 67
Ridgway, Maj Gen M.B. 49, 77
Riley, Pte Ralph G. 159
Rommel, FM Erwin 14, 36, 53, 89
Roosevelt, Brig Gen 'Teddy' 72, 73, 165, 166
Roosevelt Café, 165, *168*
Roosevelt, Capt Quentin 72
Roosevelt, President F.D. 16
Rundstedt, FM Gerd von 13, 14, 100
Russell, Pte Ken 135–7

St-Côme-du-Mont 28, *30*, 39, 40, 71, 76, 85, 86, 88, 98, 104, 108, 178–81, *179*, *180*
St-Marcouf 92, *93*, 94, *94*, 99
St-Martin-de-Varreville 27, 38, 40, 49, 69, 71, 81, 142, 162
Ste-Marie-du-Mont 26, *26*, 27, 30, 31, 38, 40, 46, 66, 68, 80, 82, 83, 83, 85, 88, 173–5, *173*, *174*
Ste-Mère-Église 28, 40, 43, 46, 47, 51, 53, 70, 78–9, 79, 85, *85*, 88, 92–4, 97, *111*, 132–9, 134, *135*, *138*, *139*; Airborne Museum 137
Samuels, Capt Joseph T. 158–9
Schlieben, *GenLt* Karl-Wilhelm von 20, 38, 43, 52, 96, 100
Shanley, Lt Col T. 77, 96, 126–7

Shettle, Capt Charles 70
Simmons, Lt Col Conrad 62
Sink, Col Robert 88, 98, 181
Soemba, HNMS 66
Staples, Pte Frank 127–8
Steele, Pte John 135–7, 135
Strayer, Lt Col Robert 71
strongpoints (Stützpunkt) 24,
   31, 89, 94, 150
Summers, Staff Sgt H. 142–6
Susan B. Anthony, SS 98

Task Force U 25, 41, 42, 55–6,
   84, 165
Taute, River 21, 24, 26, 70, 98,
   105, 107
Taylor, Maj Gen Maxwell D.
   46, 71, 88, 104, 108, 171
Tide, USS 99
Timmes, Lt Col Charles 77, 96,
   131–2
Tobruk pits 35, 39, 69
Triepel, GenMaj Gerhard 154
Turnbull, Lt Turner 140–1

US Army:
   First Army 17, 25, 89, 97
   Third Army 165
   Corps:
      V Corps 12, 31, 41, 88,
         104, 105, 106, 108, 109
      VII Corps 3, 12, 24, 40, 82,
         84, 85, 88, 104, 110
   Divisions:
      2nd Armored 109
      4th Inf 12, 40, 41, 61–2,
         65, 74, 76, 81, 82, 84,
         88, 100, 166, 170–1
      9th Inf 104
      82nd Airborne 12, 16, 17,
         40–1, 43, 45, 46–7, 50,
         70, 77, 78, 79, 83, 84,
         85, 88, 96
      90th Inf 41, 75, 82, 89, 96,
         97, 166
      101st Airborne 12, 17, 40,
         43, 44, 45, 69–71, 83, 85,
         88, 98, 99, 105, 170–1,
         176–84, 182
   Brigades:
      1st Engineer Special 74, 76,
         82, 85, 162, 166, 167
   Regiments:
      8th Inf 7, 11, 62, 67, 72,
         73, 74, 76, 80, 82, 83,
         84, 86, 92, 93, 100, 123,
         146, 167, 170
      12th Inf 74, 76, 81, 83, 94,
         100
      22nd Inf 72–3, 76, 80–1,
         83, 84, 94, 100, 158
      39th Inf 104
      175th Inf 106

US Army - Regiments cont.
      325th GIR 84, 88, 93, 96,
         100
      327th GIR 74, 86, 89, 98,
         105, 107, 108
      357th Inf 97
      359th Inf 75, 77
      401st GIR 74, 88, 96, 98,
         106, 107
      501st PIR 42–3, 46, 50,
         70–1, 79, 85, 86, 98, 108,
         176, 178
      502nd PIR 42, 42, 46, 51,
         56, 71, 72, 79, 105, 106,
         107, 109, 142–6, 183–4
      505th PIR 46, 49, 51, 77,
         78, 79, 82, 92, 93, 96,
         100, 129–30, 139–41
      506th PIR 46, 47, 50, 70,
         71, 80, 88, 98, 108,
         171–2, 178
      507th PIR 46, 47, 51, 77,
         78, 96, 125–6, 131
      508th PIR 46, 47, 51, 52,
         77, 96, 122, 123, 127
      531st Engineer Shore 74
   Battalions:
      14th Armd Field Arty 110
      29th Field Arty 83
      44th Field Arty 100
      49th Engineer Combat 80
      65th Armd Field Arty 66,
         75, 98, 106
      70th Tank 62, 74, 80, 83,
         93
      80th Airborne AAA 87
      87th Armd Field Arty 98
      87th Chemical Weapons 72
      237th Engineer Combat 62,
         73
      238th Engineer Combat 80,
         165
      299th Engineer Combat 62,
         72
      319th Glider Field Arty 87
      320th Barrage Balloon 81
      320th Glider Field Arty 87
      321st Glider Field Arty 98
      326th Airborne Engineer
         46, 106
      377th PFA 46, 51, 98
      552nd AAA/AW 160
      746th Tank 81, 81, 84, 92,
         93, 96, 98
      819th Aviation Engineer 99
      899th Tank Destroyer 81,
         94
      907th Para Field Arty 98,
         106
      1106th Engineer Combat
         Group 62, 80, 81
   Other units:
      4th Cav Sqdn 57, 84
      24th Cav Sqdn 57

US Army – Other units cont.
      29th Recon Troop 106
      286th JASC 82
      470th Amphibious Truck
         Company 97, 185
      Beach Obstacle Demolition
         Parties 62
      Howell Force 83–4, 87, 123
US Army Air Force:
      Ninth Air Force 66
      IX Tp Carrier Command 43
      52nd Tp Carrier Wing 43, 46
      53rd Tp Carrier Wing 43, 46
      92nd Tp Carrier Sqdn 137
      365th Fighter Group 157
      406th Fighter Group 165
US Coast Guard 55, 60, 166
US Navy 57, 61
      2nd Naval Beach Btn 81, 165
      Landing Craft Control 61, 67
      Minesweepers 99
      Naval Combat Demolition
         Units 62, 73
      Patrol Craft 61, 67
      Scouts and Raiders 61
      Shore Fire Control Parties 75,
         75
      Squadron VCS-7 66
Utah Beach 15, 20, 21, 24,
      64–5, 68, 72, 74, 97, 106,
      109, 119, 121, 163
      Roger White 91
      Tare Green 25, 55, 61, 62,
         67, 73
      Uncle Red 25, 61, 62, 67, 73,
         90–1

Vander Beek, Lt Howard 67
Van Fleet, Col James 62, 73, 76
Vandervoort, Lt Col 'Ben' 78,
   79
Vierville 175
Vire, River 17, 24, 51, 105,
   106, 108
Vourch, Lt Francis 151

Walters, Major Edward J 55
Ware, Pte Clarence C. 47
Warriner, 1st Lt Victor 148–9
weapons:-
   Allied:
      bazookas 100, 127–8, 146,
         158
      flamethrowers 100, 158–9
      mortars 72, 73, 146
   German:
      80-mm mortar 35, 67
      Goliath vehicles 35, 66
Wharton, Brig Gen James E. 74
Winters, Lt Richard 172–3
Winton, Lt Col W.F. 83
Wright, Pte Robert E. 176, 177
WXYZ position 38, 72, 142,
   144–6, 144, 145